D1784912

City
Transformed

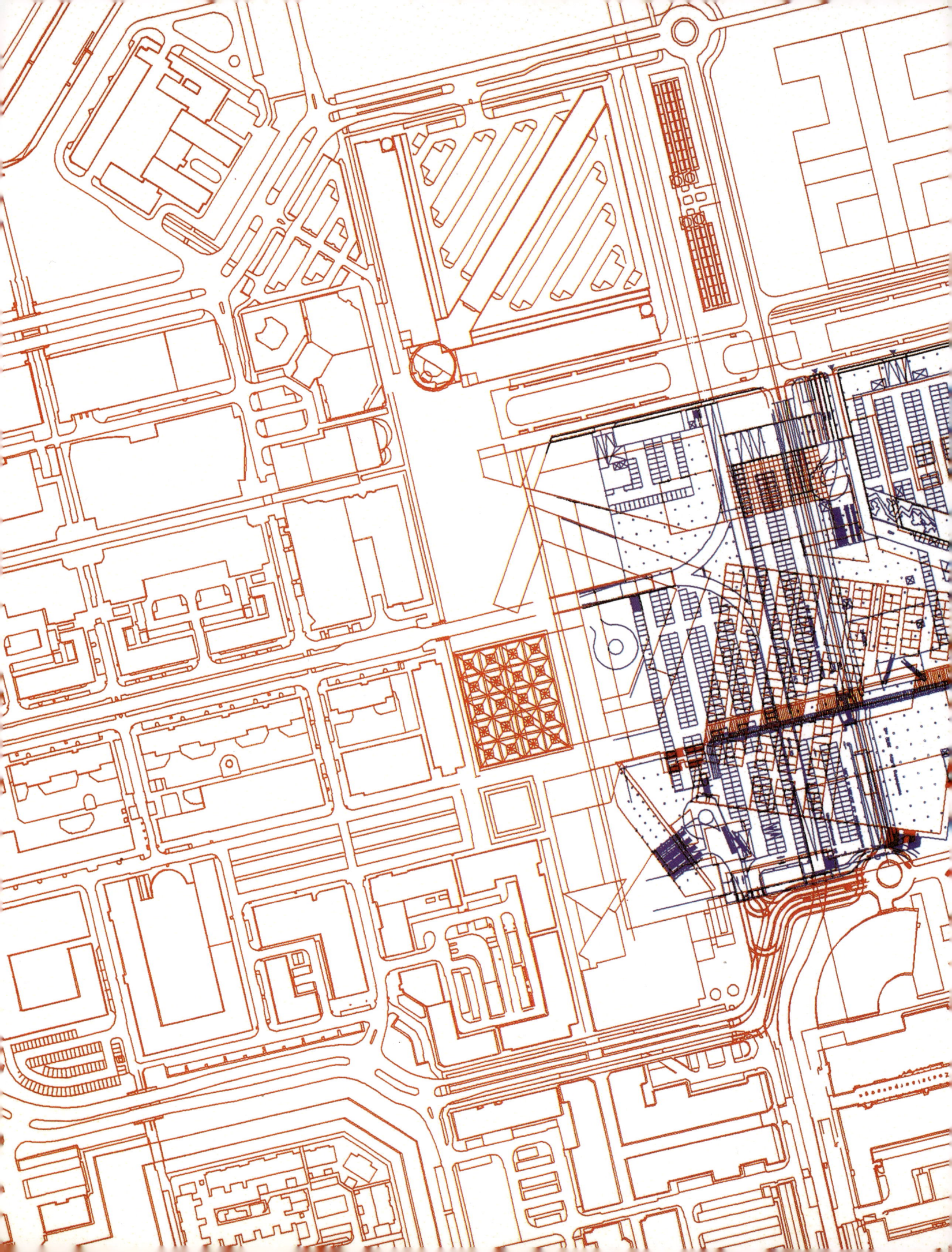

Kenneth Powell

City Transformed

Urban Architecture at the Beginning of the 21st Century

teNeues

Introduction

The future of cities is the future of the earth. The 21st century will finally confirm the fate of man as an urban being. A hundred years ago, 10 per cent of the world's population lived in cities. Well before the end of the 20th century, that proportion had risen to a half, with the world's cities growing at the rate of 250,000 every day. In 1999, the Chinese were reported to be developing 500 new towns, each planned to contain over 400,000 inhabitants. Cities, as presently conceived and managed, pose an enormous threat to the survival of humanity – 75 per cent of the pollution we generate comes from urban areas and the impetus for growth, particularly, for example, in East Asia, often overwhelms considerations of environmental protection. 'The dynamic and highly creative' urban culture of Asia can be – and is – celebrated, yet equally inspires grave misgivings in the West.[1]

Moreover, the new cities of the millennium call into question every conventional notion of what a city is or should be. China has described its new cities as 'special economic zones', arbitrarily imposed on swathes of farmland. The architect Rem Koolhaas, whose projects include a masterplan for the expansion of Hanoi, refers to 'urban systems' and has coined the term 'cities of exacerbated difference' to describe the complex and shifting phenomenon of the new Asian city-region.

The city as a threat to the civilized order is not a new idea – city life has always been seen as a challenge to social stability, not least at the time of the Industrial Revolution. Charles Dickens depicted the growth of London as a monster, devouring people in its wake. What Manchester was for the mid-19th century, Los Angeles became for the end of the 20th century, 'a maelstrom of growth and crisis', bent on social and environmental disaster.[2] The devastating riots of 1992 seemed to confirm that diagnosis.[3] Yet, no sooner had Mike Davis's terrifying vision of Los Angeles – foreshadowed in the cult film *Blade Runner* (1982) – gained wide currency than it was challenged. Charles Jencks defended Los Angeles as 'the

Honoré Daumier's nightmarish view of an overcrowded London slum - one result of the Industrial Revolution.

multicultural city with more variety of flora, fauna, lifestyles, ethnic groups and individuals doing their own thing – with more sheer difference – than any other city I know'.[4] For Jencks, no other city offered such potential for the development of the new and diverse – or 'pluralistic' – types of architecture of the late 20th century.

Architecture has been inseparably connected with the development of cities since people first banded together to live in settlements and 'civilization' – the term implies an urban existence – was born.[5] The dazzling visions of Daniel Burnham, Tony Garnier, Antonio Sant'Elia and Le Corbusier were prefigured in images of the ideal city extending back to ancient Greece and even beyond.[6] Western Classical and Judeo-Christian values underpinned Corbusier's vision of the Ville Radieuse and infused even his new capital of Chandigarh, as sure an alien imposition on India as Lutyens and Baker's New Delhi. As the North American-inspired towers of Shanghai, Hanoi, Kuala Lumpur and Jakarta confirm, the modern city is as much a product of western imperialism as any old colonial capital.

At the beginning of the 21st century, architects are confronting the challenge of the city at a time when any global consensus on what the city of the future should be and do has largely collapsed. While a North American model continues to be imposed on the

developing world, western cities are undergoing a renaissance which implies the rejection of many of the orthodoxies of the recent past. Those orthodoxies came under attack from the Sixties onwards – the pioneering urbanism of Kevin Lynch and Louis Kahn stressed the inseparability of uses and built form and a revived interest in architectural typology and urban planning (as exemplified in the work of Camillo Sitte) undermined the arrogant universalism of the International Style. The zoning policies of post-war cities and the subsequent dispersal of activity, leading to dead city centres and ever-spreading suburbs, were pilloried in an Architectural Press publication of 1971 – Civilia – which drew on the English Garden City tradition and the picturesque 'townscape' ethos developed by the *Architectural Review* to propose an intensification of urban form which would halt the spread of suburbia and rekindle city life. The assault on the Modernist city had been launched in 1961 by Jane Jacobs, whose passionate diatribe *The Death and Life of Great American Cities* was to become one of the most resonant texts of the century. Jacobs was an outsider and could be marginalized, at least for a time. The emergence of an alternative urbanism, which jettisoned the ideal city and celebrated the real city, in all its diversity and even disorder, produced the founding texts of post-Modernism – including Koetter and Colin Rowe's *Collage City* (1977) and Denise Scott Brown and Robert Venturi's *Complexity and Contradiction in Architecture* (published as early as 1966). If Venturi's stamping ground was Las Vegas, that of Aldo Rossi, whose Architecture of the City became a key text in Europe, was the historic Italian city, Milan, Turin or Genoa – indeed, the potent image of the historic city was a prime cause of the Italian reaction against Modernism, in full flow from 1960 onwards. During the 1970s the ideal city was reborn in a new form as Classical models, of a more or less literal variety, gained new currency in the work, in particular, of the Luxembourg-born polemicist Leon Krier. Krier's aim was 'the reconstruction of the European city' as a place

of mixed uses, dense occupation and traditional order. Krier's was a superficially conservative vision – he infuriated liberals by defending the work of Hitler's architect, Albert Speer – but, significantly, he reasserted the necessary connection between built form and economic and political realities and exposed the bogus radicalism of the urban polity of the post-1945 era, when the Modern Movement sold out to corporate capitalism. 'The symbolic richness of traditional architecture and city', wrote Krier, 'is based on the proximity and dialogue of the greatest possible variety of private and public uses and hence on the expression of true variety as evidenced in the meaningful and truthful articulation of public spaces, urban fabric and skyline'.[7] Krier's thinking influenced many architects who would never have considered themselves 'traditionalists' and was absorbed into mainstream thinking about urban design and city architecture. Yet more literal attempts to realise his prescriptions fell flat. What had been intended as a new hill town for 5,000 inhabitants in rural Dorset in the UK, the Prince of Wales's Poundbury, ended up as a genteel, rather twee, but also inert, retirement suburb of Dorchester. In the USA, Krier's ideas underlay the gated and fortified settlements of Seaside and Celebration, Florida, places where the very rich could turn their backs on real city life. Such

above
For some the devastating 1992 Los Angeles riots represented a confirmation of the city's urban disintegration.

right
In Tony Garnier's idealized vision of the *Cité Industrielle* the inhabitants enjoy a low-rise mixed-use industrial garden city, kept clean thanks to electricity.

places had no more significance for the urban future than the pastiche fantasy resorts of Las Vegas. A Krierite scheme for the reconstruction of the area around St Paul's Cathedral in London fell victim to commercial forces which turned it into a series of period façades applied to standard modern office blocks.

The failure of the New Classical agenda was inevitable, in that no modern city can be dragooned into the stylistic and cultural trappings of an historic past which means little or nothing to many of its inhabitants. Not only the issue of architectural style, but the substance and rationale of urban development too are subject to intense questioning and debate. The prime role of the modern city is as centre of consumption rather than production, and most recent urban architecture reflects that reality. Perhaps the only architects who can beat the system are the landmark-builders, the creators of what Rowan Moore calls 'urban Rolexes... a form of advertising, where buildings perform the role of three-dimensional, international, permanent advertisements for a city'.[8] Yet the work of these 'signature architects', the natural allies of mayors on the make, has become a commodity in its own right – bringing Frank Gehry to Bilbao, for example, to design the new Guggenheim has proved to be a very sound investment.

The new urban architecture is rooted in a great tradition in which the architect is the

proper begetter not only of buildings but equally of urban form. (It was the Renaissance theorist Leon Battista Alberti who pointed out that a building is merely a city in microcosm.) Equally, the city architecture builds on the lessons of the 20th century, absorbing the lessons of the conservationist and environmental lobbies, learning from the medical and social sciences and seeking to create not just inhabited space but liveable places – real public spaces are being created as they have not been for 50 years. Amazingly, the idea of a city as a place of enjoyment, enlightenment, a place to live – not just a place to make money – is rapidly re-emerging. So the urban being becomes once more a citizen as the purely functional idea of the city gives way to a broader view. The Barcelona architect and urbanist Josep Martorell stresses the significance of public space: 'market forces ... are particularly concerned with building-filled spaces, because their economic output can be privatized and controlled. The void, however, is the public domain which excludes nobody'. Martorell urges his fellow architects: 'we should once again adopt a belligerent attitude in favour of our fellow citizens'.[9] Architecture needs to renew its belief in itself and cease to be the passive adjunct of technological change.

Architecture cannot retreat from the city. It has to address the city of the future – which implies an acceptance of growth and change. The Utopian architect-planners of the Arts and Crafts Movement shrank from the city – the English Garden City, so widely imitated throughout Europe and North America, was the result. The pioneers of the Garden City, led by Ebenezer Howard (whose seminal book, *Tomorrow: A Peaceful Path to Real Reform*, appeared in 1898) made zoning of uses and low density the main planks of their crusade. Reducing densities was seen as the answer to every problem facing humanity, from tuberculosis to racial prejudice. The post-1945 New Towns were intended to address the issue of 'space compression' – by 1970 there were 34 of them established or designated in Britain. By the

Seventies, however, the New Town was becoming discredited. The satellite towns around Stockholm, one of the great achievements of the era of Social Democracy, were intended to be 'balanced' live/work communities, but ended up as commuter settlements. In Britain crime, racism and mental illness were as endemic to the new towns of Stevenage or Milton Keynes as to Sheffield or Manchester. By the late 1990s, low density was seen as inimical to civilized life – a viewpoint strongly expressed by Richard Rogers, whose Urban Task Force report could be seen as the founding document of a new urbanism in Britain. There was even a tendency, reflected in what Rowan Moore calls 'the new orientalism', to see the Asian megalopolis as something to be admired and welcomed, rather than as a threat to civilized life.[10]

In China, a city like Shenzen may grow from a population of zero to three million in fifteen years, creating a 'new town' of a sort that Ebenezer Howard could never have imagined. In North America and Europe, existing cities are being repaired and extended in the wake of economic and social change – which has made most old port areas redundant and left vast tracts of vacant land where once heavy industry flourished and its workers lived. Battery Park City in Manhattan, London's Canary Wharf, the major regeneration projects in the port areas of Rotterdam and Genoa and, in its more modest way, Temple Bar in Dublin are all expressions of the movement to reclaim the city for people. In Paris, the Seine Rive-Gauche project has Dominique Perrault's Bibliothèque Nationale and a new university campus as its anchors, but the former railway yard site beyond the Austerlitz station is also being developed as an office city and as a place to live, creating a rich mix of people and uses which could not be further removed from London's (so far) mono-cultural Canary Wharf. New bridge links and a new metro line have eroded the barrier – as much perceptual as physical – of the river Seine. A series of development studies by Dominique Perrault has addressed not dissimilar issues in

Richard Rogers's masterplan for Shanghai tried to impose a formal order on the city layout, but this plan was not implemented and in practice building has been both rapid and random.

other French cities – in Caen, where a huge steelworks closed down, leaving a site close to the city centre vacant, in Nantes, following the decline of the shipbuilding industry, and in Bordeaux, where the right bank of the Garonne has become the focus for recent regeneration efforts after the relocation of the wine trade from its traditional riverside warehouses to suburban sites.

The 19th-century Industrial Revolution created new cities and transformed old ones. It equally damaged and deformed the lives of the people who lived in them. The railway set its mark indelibly on the urban form of Chicago and New York, Glasgow and London. Concentrations of tracks created a steel barricade, separating one city district from another, while freight yards sprawled across many square miles of land – in London, the City was hemmed in by them. In New York, the reconstruction of Grand Central Station (1903–13) involved the creation of a new city quarter, focussed on Park Avenue, where there had once been a huge open cutting – the (electrified) trains were put underground. The pioneer 'air rights' development confirmed the supremacy of Midtown Manhattan and provided inspiration for New York's other great exemplar of urban architecture, the Rockefeller Center, yet its implications for other large cities

have been largely ignored until relatively recently. In Germany, a national programme of investment in the rail system, with a system of high-speed intercity links, has been combined with an analysis of the development potential of the areas around the big city stations.

A series of projects by the office of von Gerkan, Marg and Partners has addressed the station quarters of Stuttgart, Frankfurt and Munich. In Munich, sinking the tracks into the city's main station and developing the land on top produces a 'Metropolitan Park' three kilometres (1.9 miles) long, 120 hectares (297 acres) in area, lined with new buildings – up to 1,850,000 square metres (20 million square feet) of new office and residential space. The project includes a complete reconstruction of the station itself, with a new daylit train shed containing the tracks (sunk 37 metres/121 feet below street level) – a series of galleries contain passenger facilities. At Grand Central, the experience of boarding a train has never been pleasant – the platforms are subterranean and utilitarian, a far remove from the magnificent concourse above. When New York's other great rail terminal, Pennsylvania Station, was redeveloped in the 1960s, the entire station was sunk below ground and topped by the dismal Madison Square Garden development. Regarded from the time of its completion as a blot on the city, the 1960s Penn Station is now being superseded by a new station carved out of the adjacent Post Office building (1911 and, like the old station, a monumental Classical pile designed by McKim, Mead & White). The scheme, by David Childs of Skidmore, Owings & Merrill, combines restoration and adaptation of old fabric with bold new interventions. Moreover, it is seen as the key to the revitalization of a wide swathe of Manhattan's West Side – still in limbo following the decline of the port. A masterplan by Peter Eisenman (with Childs as collaborator) proposes a ribbon of development extending from the station to the Hudson River. In 2000, as in 1860, railways have the power to transform cities. Their potential is shown most dramatically, perhaps, in the Far East – for example, in Hong Kong, where Terry Farrell's massive Kowloon Station is seen as part of a process of 'urbanizing the airport' – a place where you can as easily check in for a flight to Los Angeles as buy a ticket to another part of the city. The Chek Lap Kok airport and Kowloon Station are part of a transport-led process of transformation in Hong Kong begun in the 1970s with the new metro system.

The late 20th-century transport revolution has almost infinite potential to reconfigure cities and urban life. Within cities, new transit systems, like the Bilbao Metro or London's Jubilee Line Extension, can dramatically regenerate hitherto rundown areas and change the whole perception of a place – transport is the key to redefining the city of the future. In Japan the Yokohama Port Terminal, designed by Foreign Office Architects, is seen not as a building but as an 'extension of the city'. The architects proposed that its roof should be used as an urban park – the area is equal to that of the Tuilleries Gardens in Paris.

The sheer power of architecture as a transforming force in the city can be seen at the micro, as much as the macro, scale. New buildings can give clear form to previously unresolved spaces. The Stadthaus (an exhibition gallery and conference centre) close to the huge

Gothic cathedral in the German city of Ulm amounts to only 929 square metres (10,000 square feet). Yet this Richard Meier project has given a civic presence to the cathedral square and is part of a project to define and enclose the irregular space, which had been devastated in the Second World War and poorly reconstructed. In a recognizably 'historic' city new interventions are frequently contentious and always problematic. Yet they can be the key to unlocking neglected urban spaces, restoring lost relationships, and facilitating the adaptation of historic fabric to new uses: the new urban environment – certainly in Europe – is usually a mix of old and new. In the Spanish city of Murcia, Rafael Moneo's new town hall is a striking example of how contemporary design can, in one move, complete an historic entity. Another Meier project, the Museum of Contemporary Art in Barcelona, has, for example, a dynamic role to play in the regeneration of a previously poor and decayed area of the city. In London, the conversion by Herzog & de Meuron of the former Bankside Power Station (a monumental form designed by Sir Giles Scott and completed as late as the 1960s) into the Tate Gallery's museum of modern art (Tate Modern) has not only provided a new use for an undervalued building. It has forged a new identity, Bankside, for a previously ill-defined stretch of Southwark riverside. The decision to retain the power station and adapt it (and in relatively conservative fashion), rather than to tear down or radically recast the building may prove to be one of the strengths of the project, since Bankside's rigorously industrial image seems to appeal equally to artists and to the gallery-going public.

There is nothing new about the idea of culture as an engine of regeneration – London's South Bank Centre (on the site of the 1951 Festival of Britain) was a 1960s move to shift the focus of London's arts industries across the Thames. (It did not entirely work, largely because communications were poor and also because the Centre was a thin strip of

development, isolated both from South London and from the 'real' London where pubs and restaurants sustained West End theatregoers.) London's Barbican Centre was also deliberately positioned in a redeveloped area, seen as needing an element of liveliness – the Centre subsequently suffered from the same problems that affected the South Bank.

More radical was the Parc de la Villette, one of the Parisian *grands projets* which placed a new science museum, music college, auditorium and landscaped park in a rundown site (previously housing the city's abattoirs) far from the centre of the capital. At the beginning of the 21st century, cultural enterprises are likely to be firmly linked to a broader regeneration agenda, as in the former docklands of Manchester and Salford, where Daniel Libeskind's northern branch of the Imperial War Museum looks set to join Michael Wilford's Lowry Centre at the heart of a new waterside city district.

In contrast, the recently (1999) completed reconstruction of London's Royal Opera House looks conservative – in essence, it provides new facilities for the performers, staff and audiences of an old-established theatre that has itself remained little changed. However, the project (by Dixon Jones BDP), though dating in its essentials from the mid-Eighties, remains

provocative and controversial. Retrenching the ROH in Covent Garden meant squeezing out local businesses and residents from parts of the site. The urban approach adopted, with its roots in the polemics of Rowe, Krier and Rossi, was out of step with the conventions of the 1990s – its frank acceptance of the need for urban collage and picturesque composition marked out its architects as prime practitioners of that tradition. The new ROH is a megastructure, yet it is made to look like a mixed city quarter. The diversity of the city is celebrated.

It is the acceptance of diversity – the reassertion of heterogeneity of city life – which characterizes the new urban architecture. Yet the key to the city of the future is that it is a place where people live – and live near their work. Zoning was a strategy to separate people – or at least the well-off – from the effects of polluting industries. In North American and western European cities, those industries are defunct and the same inexorable process of change will clear them from the cities of eastern Europe, Asia and Latin America. Glasgow's East End, for example, was ravaged by industrialization. First, the rich moved out, then the slums were torn down. Now it is the East End which hosts Glasgow's Homes for the Future experiment – an experiment so successful that it is likely to be repeated on many other sites.

Housing is fundamental to a viable city – a city where nobody lives is dead. (Northern Europeans have always admired the cities of Italy and Spain, where 'ordinary' people still live in the historic cores, yet this is no accident – planning policies have kept it that way.) Housing is also the area where the Modern Movement strove most vigorously against historic urban patterns – and failed. The high-rise housing projects of Pruitt-Igoe in the US and Ronan Point in Britain became symbols of that failure. In reaction, post-Modernists advocated the revival of the traditional urban pattern of streets, squares and urban blocks and, on occasion, of traditional styles of housing – hence the Poundbury Farm/Seaside syndrome.

The street was the starting point for the IBA (Internationale Bauausstellung) projects of the 1980s in Berlin. The new IBA was a pointed retort to that of the 1950s, which had produced the CIAM-inspired Hansa Viertel quarter – towers and slabs in a grassy park. Rob Krier, Aldo Rossi, Hans Kollhoff and Hans Hollein were amongst the design team – all were critics of Modernism. A similar philosophy of repair inspired the London housing schemes of the 1970s and early 1980s by Jeremy Dixon. Only at the very end of the 20th century did a pragmatic and definitively modern housing architecture emerge in Britain with the work of Ian Ritchie, Allford Hall Monaghan Morris, Lifshutz Davidson and others. Elsewhere, in the

Netherlands, for example, housing was inherent to a modern view of the city. Building on a tradition of modern design (and social architecture) which extends back to the 1920s, the present generation of Dutch architects are building urban housing on a scale far beyond the experimental. In the new town of Almere, close to Amsterdam, two IBA type projects, beginning in 1990, gave architects the opportunity to design innovative housing within the masterplan of the growing settlement. Built schemes of the 1990s in Amsterdam included the Haasseweg development by Mecanoo (380 houses in a low-rise, garden city format) and the far larger Nieuw-Sloten, including a mix of low and high-rise housing. In Rotterdam, the massive Kop van Zuid regeneration project includes housing by, among others, Cepezed, F.J. van Dongen, Mecanoo, and DKV. The new Dutch housing aesthetic is as adaptable to infill sites in old towns as to city-edge locations – Erick van Egeraat's recent housing in Tilburg is a model of confident contextualism.

The new urban architecture is not about appearances but about substance, about a holistic interaction of aesthetics, politics and finance. In recent decades, the masterplan has again come to the fore – but Michelangelo, Palladio, John Nash and the Woods (of Bath)

were all masterplanners. The rise of town planning as a distinct discipline during the 20th century was part of a progressive, Modernist agenda, but even as the planners were gaining a hold in Britain, in the context of the post-war rush to reconstruction, Sir John Summerson was expressing his fears about the rise of 'a new combative attitude of mind better able to destroy than to create'.[11] For three decades, planners and architects worked mostly in harmony. When public confidence in their joint achievements collapsed, the time had come for a reconsideration of their roles.

Modern planning was rooted in political, social and economic prescriptions and developed into a pseudo-science whereby the city could be monitored, regulated, adjusted like a machine – all that was needed was the correct formula, the right mix of ingredients. This analysis proved sadly flawed. The net result of modern planning was the devastation of the traditional city and the accelerated growth of suburbia. The 30-year hegemony of Robert Moses in New York began heroically and ended in bathos. Moses's agenda was paternalistic and autocratic. On the Lower East Side, 'in a matter of a few years, the mean if lively streets of a vital slum gave way to an impersonal parkified nowhere realm punctuated by repetitious, banal housing blocks'.[12] Norman Mailer (writing in

left
The Yokohama Port Terminal in Japan is seen as an extension of the city, complete with a rooftop park.

right
Richard Meier's Statdhaus at Ulm, Germany, sensitively complements the Gothic cathedral opposite.

1963) summed up the results of the city's new housing programme as 'an architectural plague'.[13] Moses succeeded in partly devastating Greenwich Village, but the warehouse district of SoHo, already being colonized by artists, withstood the assault – and its regeneration produced the first examples of a characteristic late 20th-century housing type, the loft. By the 1970s, the preservation movement in New York was gaining in power and influence in the wake of the Penn Station disaster. Preservationists and architectural historians were to move into the void left by the discrediting of planning in the USA and Britain. A concern for history was one of the hallmarks of the new urbanism emerging in the 1970s – the Nolli Plan of Rome became an icon. The preservationists and historians – Maurice Culot in France, for example, Marcus Binney in Britain and Paolo Portoghesi in Italy – along with influential critics such as Ada Louise Huxtable and Michael Sorkin, increasingly acted as monitors of quality and social responsibility. With planners in retreat, the temptation was for developers and their architects to assume the planning role: who was to defend the public interest? In 1980s Britain, as the sagas of Paternoster Square and Canary Wharf made clear, the answer to that question was unclear. In London, with city-wide government swept away in the 1980s, it was left to bodies like English Heritage to assume a strategic role. In Berlin, in contrast, the city took a strong lead, so much so that the formalist predilections of city planning supremo Hans Stimmann – exemplified in the flabby reconstruction of the Friedrichstrasse – were compared, somewhat unfairly, to those of Albert Speer in the 1930s and 1940s. (Stimmann's insistence on the urban block infuriated radicals such as Daniel Libeskind, but was in line with the general practice of the 1980s.) In Paris, the public authorities (city/department/region/central government) took a clear lead in the masterplanning process via the APUR (Atelier Parisien d'Urbanisme) agency, which was responsible for developing the overall masterplan for Seine Rive-Gauche and developing an admirable system of competitions for areas in the city. Paris's pioneering architecture and urbanism centre, the Pavillon de l'Arsenal, set a standard which few cities could match, even by the end of the 20th century, exhibiting development proposals and arranging regular symposia and debates at which the proposals could be subjected to professional and public criticism as part of the planning process.

If a widening of democratic involvement and a concern to balance bigger agendas (employment, national prestige, social progress) against the interests of individuals and minorities was a feature of western cities by the end of the century, the new cities of the Pacific Rim seemed to be designed to crush individualism in their pursuit of sheer scale. If all the world's city dwellers lived at the densities typical in East Asian cities, claimed David Clark, they could be accommodated in an area the size of Germany – 1 per cent of the world's land mass. But the alternative to the alarming densities of Shanghai or Mexico City seemed to be increasingly the sprawling 'edge cities' flippantly embraced by modish commentators but actually part of a growing trend towards social fragmentation and the institutionalization of poverty.[14] It was left to architects – for example Toyo Ito and Richard Rogers in their unrealized Shanghai masterplans – to assert the value of the public, civic realm. Kisho Kurokawa, Ken Yeang and Norman Foster have embodied progressive environmental thinking in their work. Other western architects, such as Cesar Pelli, author of the notorious, high-energy Petronas Towers in Kuala Lumpur, were content to celebrate affluence secured at the expense of local populations and the natural environment.

The role of the urban architect at the start of a new millennium can be that of a god-like disposer, who sweeps away mountains, raises islands from the sea and moves whole populations as if they were pawns. It can equally be that of a salvage merchant, economically pulling together the resources of

left
The new town hall at Murcia, in Spain, successfully demonstrates how contemporary design can complete a historic area.

right
The Parc de la Villette was a radical attempt to transform a previously rundown site on the edge of Paris.

a place and building on them to create a viable city quarter – an area like Dublin's Temple Bar would be bulldozed in a day without a second thought in Shanghai or Jakarta. If Temple Bar exemplifies the art of urban salvage, the work of the West Coast architect Jon Jerde is about urban decoration and make-believe. From beginnings in the retail and entertainment sector, Jerde's practice has developed an expertise at creating places – of a kind – out of the unpromising interstices in the modern city. Jerde talks about 'editing' cities, creating a collage from scratch – as at Canal City Hakata, where an instant leisure and retail quarter has been slotted into a desolate riverside site on the edge of the town centre. According to Frances Anderton, Jerde 'has synthesized fantasy, commerce, entertainment and public life in a way that forces us to rethink what constitutes urban space'.[15]

'Urban truth is in the flow', wrote Spiro Kostof. Change is endemic to city life – people come to cities to be free, get richer, achieve happiness. Not all succeed, but the pragmatic definition of the city of the 16th-century philosopher, Giovanni Botero, still holds good: 'a congregation drawn together to the end that they may thereby the better live at their ease in wealth and plenty'.[16] The ideal city will never exist, but cities continue to exercise their spell. Cities are more than collections of buildings and the spaces between them, but urban architecture forms the context to the way we live and determines our destinies. Architects are the makers of the cities of the future and civilization is literally in their hands.

1 *Cities on the Move: Urban Chaos and Global Change* (London, 1999): the book of an exhibition touring to various centres in Europe and North America between 1997 and 1999 is an example of celebration.

2 *Ibid*, p.10

3 Mike Davis, *City of Quartz: Excavating the future in Los Angeles* (London, 1992), p.7

4 Charles Jencks, *Heteropolis: Los Angeles, the Riots and the Strange Beauty of Hetero-Architecture* (London, 1993), p.107

5 See, for example, Peter Hall, *Cities in Civilization* (London, 1998)

6 Helen Rosenau, *The Ideal City in its Architectural Evolution* (London, 1959)

7 Leon Krier, 'Tradition, Modernity, Modernism: Some necessary explanations', in *Architectural Design*, 57 (1987), p.43

8 Rowan Moore (ed.), *Vertigo: the Strange New World of the Contemporary City* (London, 1999), p. 43

9 Introduction to I. de Sola-Morales and X. Costa (eds), *Present and Futures: Architecture in Cities* (Barcelona, 1996), p.7

10 Moore, *op. cit.*, p.28

11 John Summerson, *Georgian London* (London, 1945), p.279

12 R.A.M. Stern, T. Mellins, D. Fishman, *New York 1960: Architecture and Urbanism Between the Second World War and the Bicentennial* (New York, 1995), p.136

13 *Ibid.*, p.79

14 P. Zellner, *Pacific Edge: Contemporary Architecture on the Pacific Rim* (London, 1998), pp.114–15

15 F. Anderton et al, *You Are Here: The Jerde Partnership International* (London, 1999), p.4

16 S. Kostof, *The City Assembled: The Elements of Urban Form through History* (London, 1992), pp.7, 305

left
Ushida Findlay's design for public housing from Glasgow's successful Homes for the Future experiment.

right
The artist Lowell Nesbitt stands atop his 1970s studio in Greenwich Village. This re-used nineteenth-century police stable is an early example of a downtown New York loft conversion.

Healing
the
City

The history of cities in the 20th century has been frequently tragic. The Second World War left major cities like Berlin, Frankfurt, Dresden, Rotterdam, Hiroshima, Tokyo, Genoa and the City of London in total or partial ruin. The rapidity with which urban routines were re-established in these places is a testimony to the inherent strength of the city. Yet it was to be decades before the damage done by warfare was fully repaired. The last bombsite in the City of London was filled only in the late 1990s. Only after the fall of the Wall did the reconstruction of Berlin start in earnest. Rotterdam's post-1945 rebuilding was heroic in scale, yet too often mundane in quality and inhumane in its effects. Only at the end of the 20th century is Rotterdam realizing the potential of modern architecture.

The post-war period was, at least in Europe, the golden era of all-embracing plans and planning legislation, part of a movement, altruistic and idealistic in origin, to create a new, more just and more rationally directed society. Decentralization, the zoning of activities and the reduction of densities were the main planks of this programme of radical reform. The new planned society found common cause with the architectural programme promoted by the Congrès Internationale d'Architecture Moderne (CIAM), its roots in the urban visions of Le Corbusier - seen most frighteningly in the Plan Voisin for Paris. The latter remained unrealized, but many such visions did come to reality. Whole districts were demolished and their populations transported. Today, the task is, in effect, to re-create the dense, mixed-use city of the past. The campaign of urban renaissance preached, for example, by Richard Rogers in Britain is effectively a crusade against the Modern Movement city. In some instances - London's Covent Garden, Paris's Marais, and Dublin's Temple Bar, for example - the reversal of public policy came in time to avoid irreparable destruction. The task was then one of repair, infill and adjustment. Elsewhere, architects have had to begin the job of rebuilding the waste places.

Urban clearance was not only a European phenomenon - in New York, the long reign of planning supremo Robert Moses saw historic neighbourhoods felled for housing projects and new roads separating one neighbourhood from another. In other American cities, the growth of central business districts forced out resident populations. A *cordon sanitaire* of rail yards and industry separated city centres from residential suburbs. When the old industries failed, those cities were left with empty wastelands surrounding their cores. If the wounds of war could be healed and the mistakes of planners corrected, the effects of economic change seemed to be inexorable and more catastrophic in their impact than any number of bombs. Dockland areas that had hummed with activity and employed many thousands degenerated into deserts and were left to rot as new container ports opened miles from the city centres of Liverpool, Rotterdam, London and Genoa. Only in the 1970s, notably with the pioneering waterfront projects in Boston and Baltimore was the potential of such areas for new uses, chiefly connected to leisure and retailing, understood. Genoa's waterfront renaissance, masterplanned by Renzo Piano, has brought the old port back to life as workplace and place of recreation.

Finally, as in the case of Kobe, natural disasters can still wreck cities. Lisbon, which rebuilt itself after an earthquake in the 18th century, led the way in demonstrating how such a disaster can actually lead to real renewal. A less sweeping disaster, the great Chiado fire, has ironically allowed Lisbon to reclaim its old heartland, which had been in steady decline for decades.

The process of urban repair calls on all the skills of the architect. The repair and reuse of old buildings is often a key element. Elsewhere, it is a case of inserting new fabric into the gap left by war, disaster, neglect or deliberate destruction. Glasgow's Homes for the Future project, completed in 1999 as part of the city's Year of Architecture festival, is an exemplary instance of how modern design can be both innovative and contextual. If planning half-killed the traditional city, it is increasingly the task of architecture to resurrect it.

DALLAS
Victory District

(1999-   )

Dallas today appears to illustrate all the problems identified by Jane Jacobs in *The Death and Life of Great American Cities* – an over-developed central business district, full of gas-guzzling skyscrapers, which gives way to huge tracts of dereliction and post-industrial blight, scattered with housing for the poor and forming a barrier between the city and the affluent suburbs beyond.

Koetter Kim's masterplan for the Victory District began with an analysis of the city which revealed, however, that Dallas possesses a more complex and interesting urban form than might be imagined. The central area of the city consists of a series of distinct quarters – the central business district, the West End (now a designated Historic District), the Market Center and the 24-hectare (60-acre) Arts District, claimed as the largest cultural quarter in the USA. Unfortunately, these areas are separated by swathes of rail tracks and freight yards and by urban freeways.

Developing the Victory District is seen as a way of linking together these core districts and giving central Dallas more of a unity. The site, 26 hectares (65 acres) in extent, is bounded by the Stemmons Freeway and the edge of the West End. Once it was a vibrant industrial quarter. Now it is largely cleared of buildings, except for a huge, redundant power station.

'Victory represents one of the last great opportunities to shape the life and landscape of a great American city', claim Koetter Kim. Their masterplan proposes a mixed-use (office, residential, retail, entertainment, hotel and leisure), street-oriented, largely pedestrian environment – Koetter Kim see their proposals as a framework for development, rather than a set of rigid guidelines. The basis of this framework is, in essence, a series of city blocks which address the street but these are offered as 'building parcels' with latitude for potential developers to divide or combine these parcels to suit their particular needs. A pattern of open spaces is proposed, threading through the new district. Density and height of buildings is envisaged as increasing towards the northern

top right
The American Airlines Center Plaza provides a generous outdoor public space with eating facilities.

right
Koetter Kim's masterplan for the Victory District of Dallas (far right and centre) addresses the fragmentation of the city and seeks to link together disparate urban quarters with a new mixed-use district including cultural, business and leisure facilities and public spaces (top right).

bottom right
The city's fragmentation is the result of 19th-century railway development and the construction of urban freeways in the 20th century.

left
Dallas's ring of derelict industrial and railway land, circling the business district, is typical of large American cities.

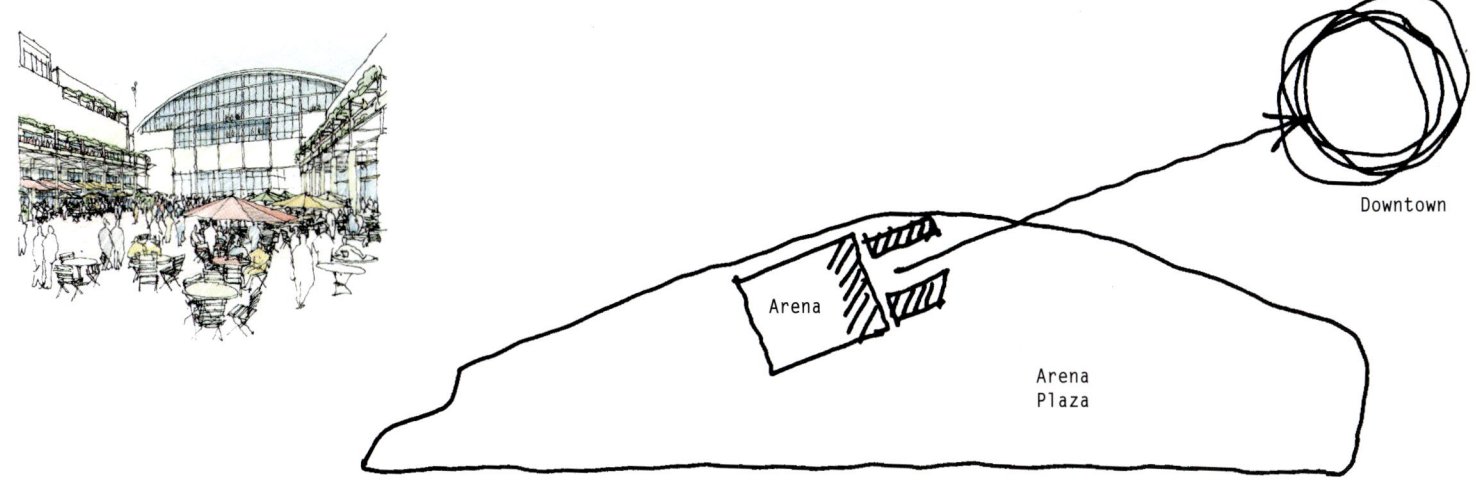

Arena

Arena
Plaza

Downtown

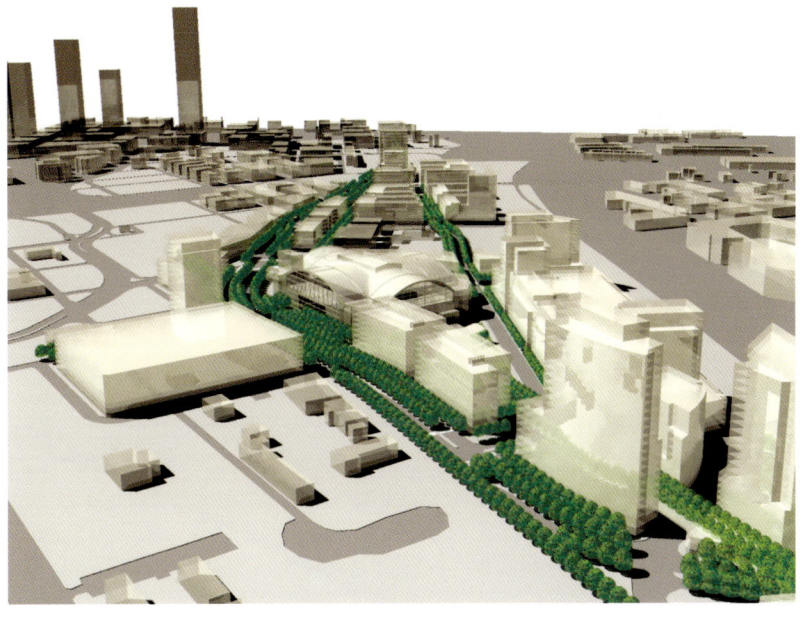

portion of the site – to the south, medium-rise blocks are in tune with the character of the old West End. To the north, there is perceived potential for high buildings. A variety of street formats is proposed, with main streets featuring shops at ground level.

The architectural form of the development could be quite diverse, ranging from three-storey row houses of traditional appearance to office blocks of up to 30 storeys with floorplates of around 1,858 square metres (20,000 square feet). A strong emphasis is placed on the streetwall and the development of façades which read as three distinct zones – base, middle and top, implying a generally solid architecture. Indeed, brick and stone are laid down as the usual facade materials. Arcades are used on certain blocks to provide respite from the Texan sun (and, on occasions, rain). Architectural style, as such, is not seen as an issue – Richard Meier could as easily work here as Robert M. Stern.

The project is, however, informed by a post-modern concern for building typology and hierarchy and by a passionate conviction that the traditional street is the basis of city life. As such, it offers a well-tested (see, for example, Battery Park City, pages 132–41) and popular antidote to the fragmentation typical of the North American city.

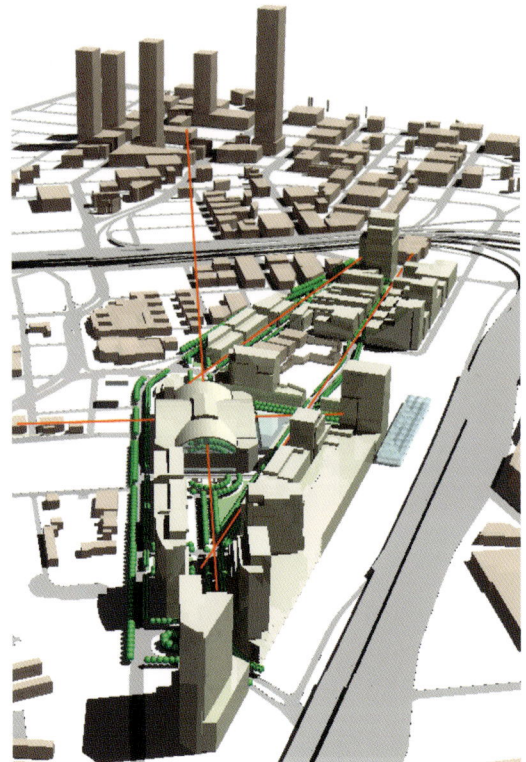

left, top and bottom
The scale of the new buildings varies, but traditional hardwearing materials, brick and stone, are specified while the classic urban street is the basis of the plan.

left
The chasms formed by rail yards are infilled with 'over the tracks' development.

right
The traditional city block is fundamental to the masterplan, shown in the model (top) and the numbered block plan (centre), which envisages phased development over a 24-hectare (60-acre) area of inner Dallas (illustrated in the bottom four plans).

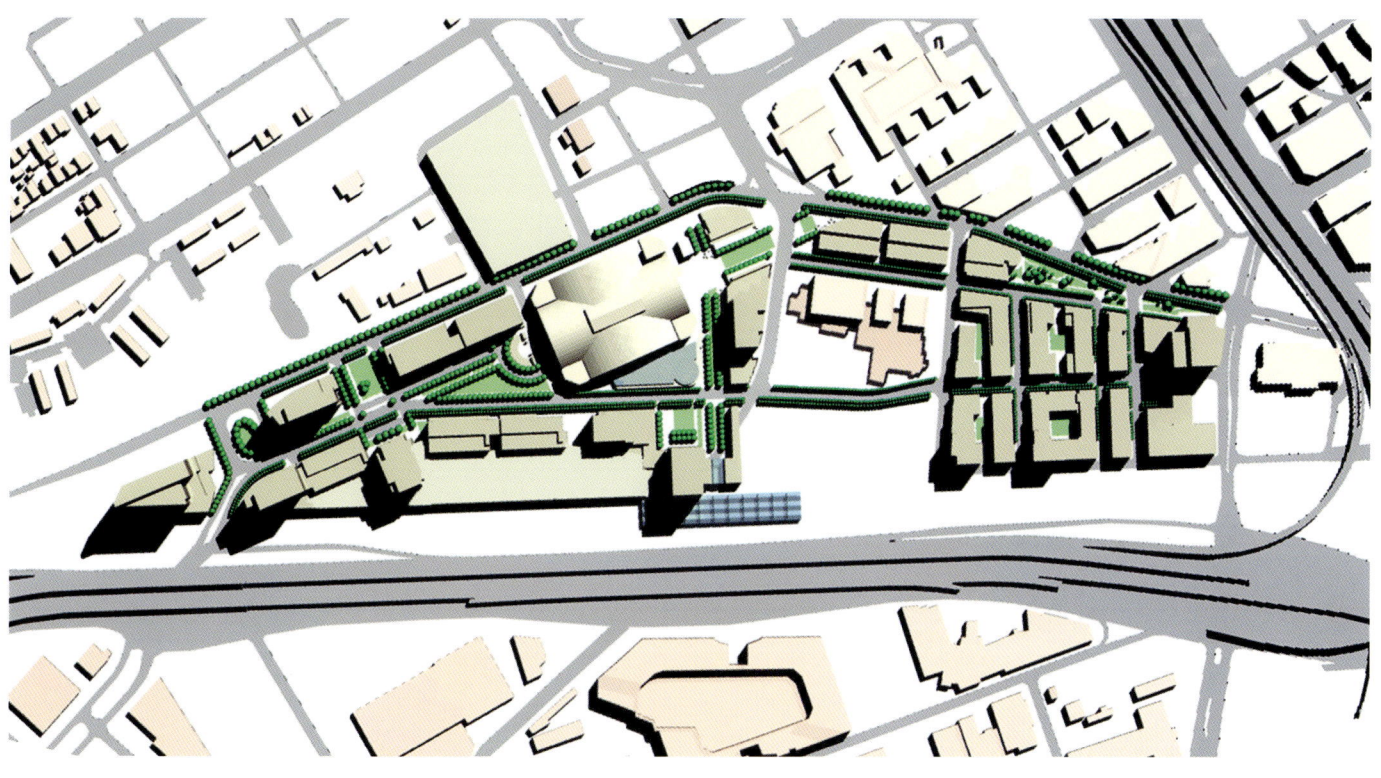

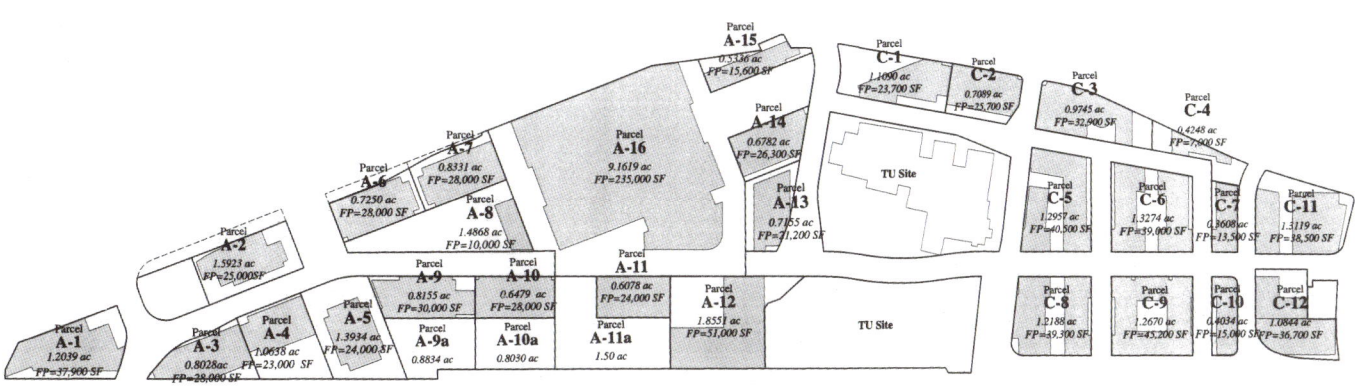

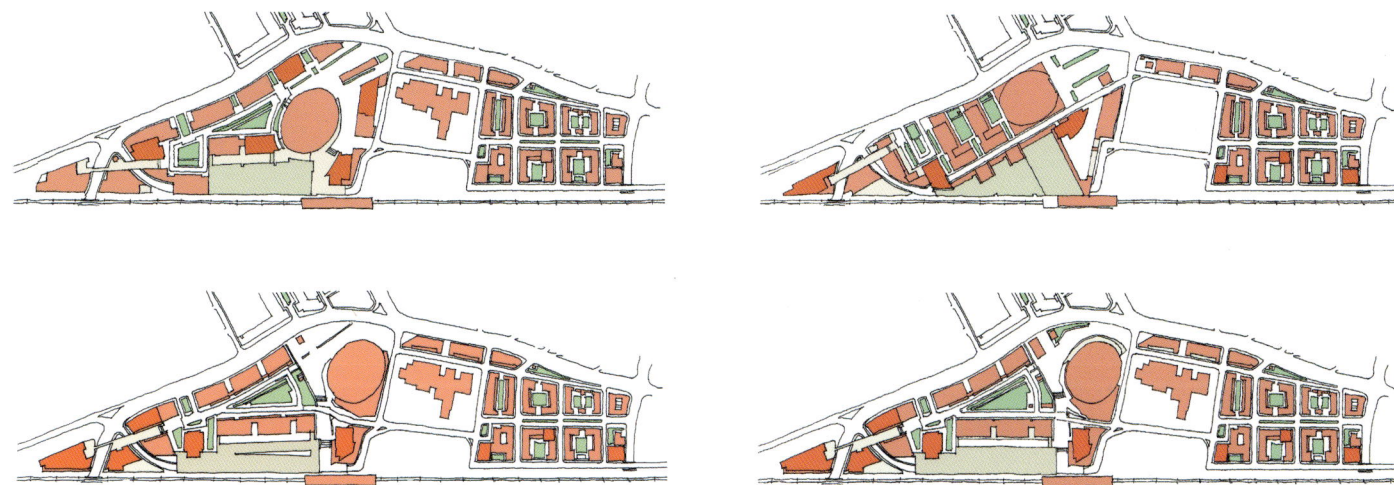

SEATTLE
City centre
regeneration
projects

(1997-   )

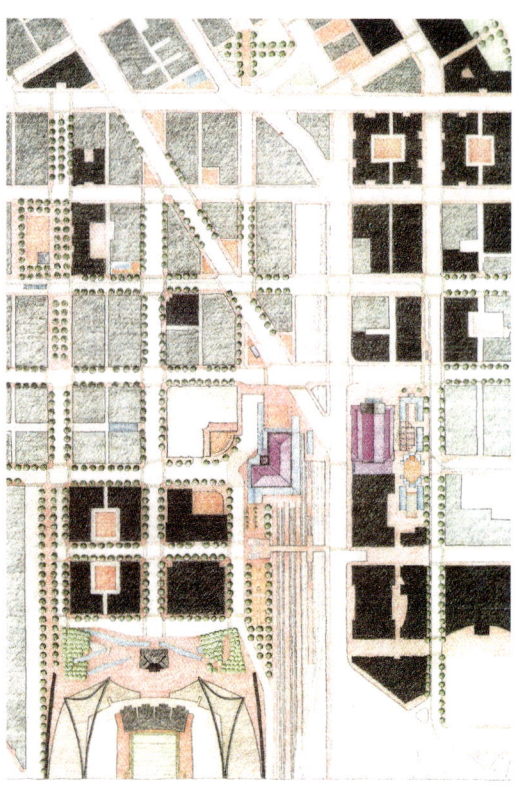

Though reckoned one of the most 'liveable' of American cities and the centre of a region that has experienced a staggering 30 per cent population increase in 20 years, Seattle has not been immune to the decay that has hit many other large city centres in the USA since the 1950s. The closure of two big department stores in the downtown area as recently as the early Nineties was a severe blow to its fortunes, yet downtown Seattle has sprung back – since 1998, over 100 construction projects have been completed there, begun or announced, evidence of a real development boom which continues throughout the city. During 1997, $1 billion worth of building permits were issued. During 1998, the figure was nearer $1.25 billion and a substantial proportion of this investment is going into the central area.

Much of the credit for Seattle's renaissance has to be given to the partnership of public and private enterprise led by Mayor Paul Schell (elected in 1997). Schell campaigned for inner-city revival and the limiting of suburban sprawl – a programme in tune, interestingly, with that of the Urban Task Force in Britain – and promoted the idea that good architecture is vital to regeneration. Schell has found a powerful ally in Paul Allen, sometime partner in Microsoft turned developer/philanthropist and the initiator of a number of key projects, including the eagerly awaited $100 million Experience Music Center designed by Frank Gehry. (Initial studies for the building, set to have something of the impact of the Bilbao Guggenheim when it opens in 2000, involved forms derived from a deconstructed guitar...) Allen's investment in the city's cultural and leisure industries is acting as a catalyst to encourage other developers to invest in Seattle. The new $425 million, 72,000-seat football stadium, due for completion in 2002 and designed by Ellerbee Becket is being built by a public/private partnership with Allen as lead player. Nearby in the South Downtown area is the site for the new Safeco baseball stadium (designed by NBBJ, with 47,000 seats, cost: $500 million), a state-of-the-art venue with

top right
Frank Gehry's Experience Music Center is likely to become the centrepiece of Seattle's urban renaissance and to rival his Bilbao Guggenheim as a tour de force of structure and form making.

right
An overall view of the proposed project shows how King Street Station (1906), with its landmark tower, becomes part of a major public transport interchange as an element of Seattle's campaign of downtown regeneration. The plan also shows the recycled Union Street Station

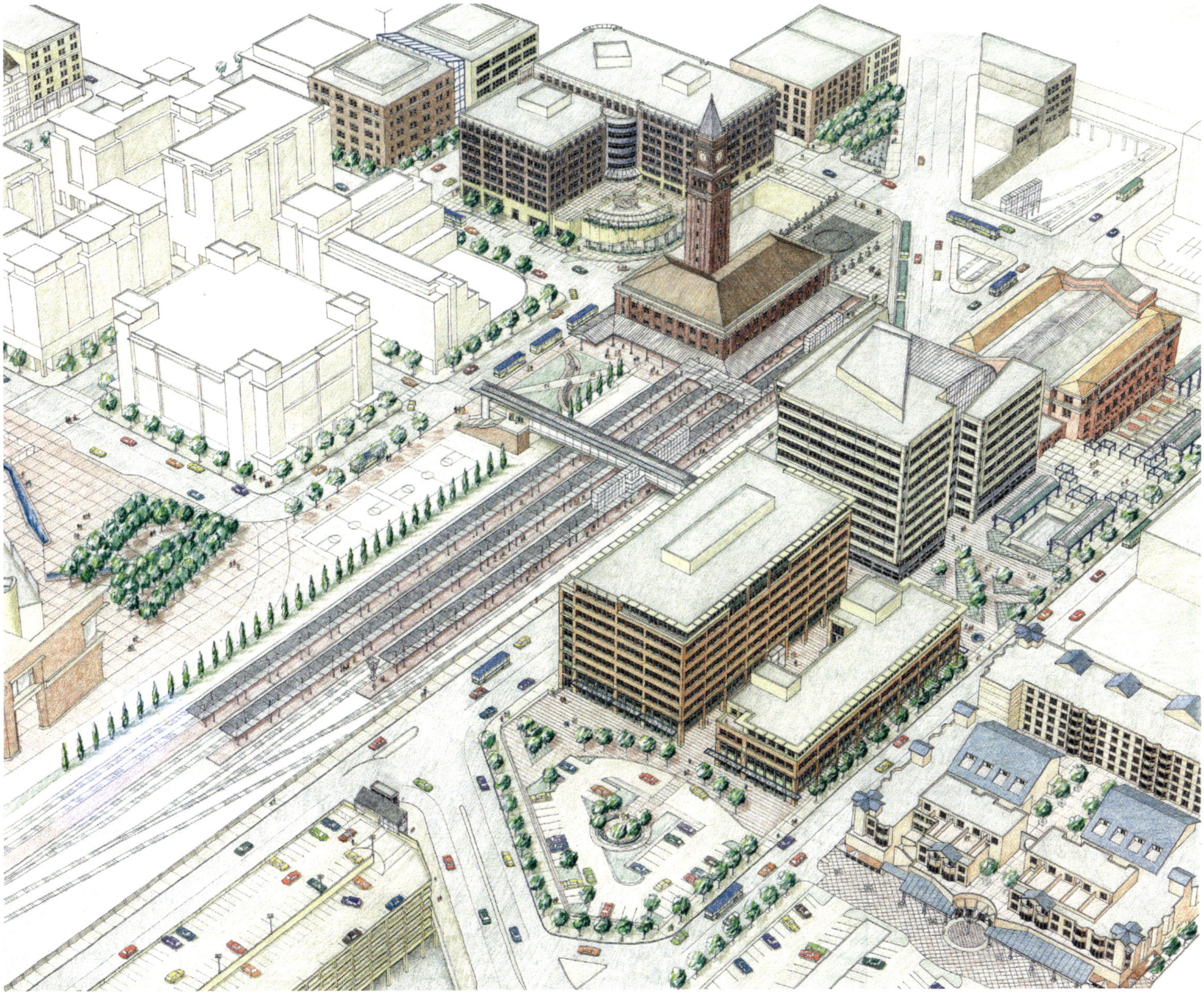

top left and above
The redundant 1912
Union Street Station
is to be renovated,
with a new landmark
office building by
Peter Pran of NBBJ
Architects on
adjacent land.

bottom left and below
The new Safeco
baseball stadium,
designed by NBBJ
Architects, is one of
two major new sports
facilities in central
Seattle.

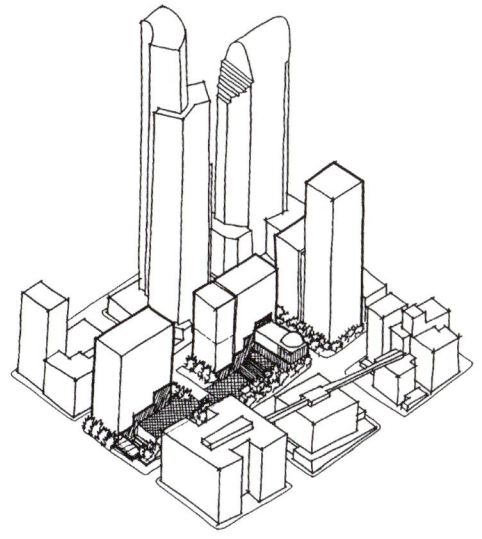

above
Seattle's civic
centre is being
expanded to a
masterplan by Hewitt
Architects/Weinstein
Copeland.

right
The Millennium Tower
by Zimmer Gunsul
Frasca Partnership.

retractable roof and a home for the Seattle Mariners – Allen is an ardent fan. The stadium replaces the enclosed Kingdome of the 1960s. Construction began in 1999. Few cities in the world can boast two stadia of this standard.

Allen's Vulcan Northwest development arm is renovating the redundant 1912 Union Station (closed in 1971), and adding a 27,000-square-metre (290,000-square-foot) office block designed by Peter Pran of NBBJ – a powerful new landmark structure for Seattle. The refurbished station will house the new headquarters of Seattle Transit, the body running the region's new commuter light-rail network.

King Street Station (1906 by Reed & Stem) has remained in use, though it has suffered from unsympathetic alterations and general neglect. It is being renovated as a major transport interchange used by intercity (Amtrak) and commuter trains and the new commuter rail services as well as buses. The historic structure will be faithfully restored in line with proposals drawn up by Otak Ltd and Hardy Holzman Pfeiffer Associates. Within 20 years, it is envisaged that the number of rail travellers using the station will increase tenfold.

Seattle has never possessed the major civic monuments typical of other front-rank American cities. This deficiency is being remedied – Robert Venturi's Art Museum was completed some time ago, a new US Courthouse is due for completion in 2003, while the new Central Library project, also due for completion in 2003, has been awarded to Rem Koolhaas. Most significantly, the city is replacing the present motley collection of municipal premises with a new civic centre (designed by Hewitt Architects, with Weinstein Copeland). The new city hall, municipal courthouse and police headquarters will be connected by areas of public space, external and internal, and gardens – public space is seen as the key to the project, which aims to create a civic centre visibly open to the voters. The location is equally significant, on the edge of the South Downtown regeneration area.

Public investment is acting as a catalyst to attract the private sector – the perception is that Seattle is now a booming market place for retailing, office space and residential development.

The Pacific Place development, according to architects NBBJ, looks for inspiration to the old-style downtown areas of the past 'when downtowns had interesting storefronts and canopies, numerous store entrances and trees lining the street'. The 31,000-square-metre (335,000-square-foot) development contains shops, restaurants and a multiplex cinema. The architecture is relatively modest, but designed to reflect the character of adjacent buildings, such as the former Frederick & Nelson department store, a victim of the early Nineties recession but now stylishly renovated for retailer Nordstrom by Callison Architecture. Callison's One Convention Place scheme (1998–2000; 28,000 square metres/300,000 square feet of offices) marks the revival of the Seattle office market and forms part of an expansion plan for the Washington State Convention and Trade Center, seen as a vital investment in the future. The aesthetic of the building is entirely contemporary – a shot in the arm for matter-of-fact Seattle and a refreshing contrast to the neo-Deco of much recent commercial

left
The Harbor Steps
development creates
a new public route
to the ocean and
includes a series of
residential towers,
plus hotel, retail
and leisure
facilities, close to
the recent art museum
designed by Venturi
Scott Brown (visible
at the top of the
steps behind the
statue).

above, *right and
below*
Seattle is building
on the established
success of its
revived waterfront,
with projects
involving both
renovation and
new-build.

architecture in the USA. (Callison's 426-room W Seattle Hotel, which opened in autumn 1999 and is the first new-build hotel in the city for over 15 years, takes the form of a cut-off Art Deco skyscraper.)

Seattle's residential market is booming, with record price rises (20 per cent in a year) for houses and apartments. There is a clear danger that even middle-income families will be pushed out of the city, but Mayor Schell's housing agenda is encouraging (through tax breaks and other incentives) the development of low-cost housing in the downtown area as part of a policy of intensifying the density of the city. Around 2,000 downtown residential units are currently in the pipeline. Probably the most interesting development is Hewitt Architects' Harbor Steps, located close to the Art Museum and the recently constructed Benaroya Symphony Hall. The scheme takes advantage of the steep slope of the site to create a new pedestrian route towards the ocean – the Harbor Steps, designed by Arthur Erickson. Some 800 rented apartments are planned in four towers, which also accommodate a hotel, shops, libraries, leisure facilities and other amenities. Mixed use is combined with a blend of private and public space – the aim was to avoid the ghetto-like ethos of some city centre residential developments.

Seattle has many assets that other cities might envy – location, scale, high-profile industries, an affluent and highly skilled population – and it is also it is building on them in a way which commands attention. The architectural legacy of the 1990s/2000s boom will be diverse – but perhaps this is the right way. Seattle needs some striking new monuments, but the task it has been addressing is also one of repair and renovation. The mix looks promising.

above
The extension of the Swedish Medical Center campus is another major city centre project by NBBJ.

left
Callison Architects' One Convention Place project, completed in 2000, marked the revival of the office market in downtown Seattle.

top right
The expansion of Seattle/Tacoma International Airport (by NBBJ Architects) reflects the growing strength of the city as a business centre.

right
The headquarters of Teledesic (NBBJ Architects) are housed in a reused 1970s warehouse, where much of the industrial feel has been maintained.

BERLIN
Potsdamer Platz

(1991-2000)

Just as Norman Foster's Reichstag and the new government quarter around the Spreebogen is the symbol of Berlin's political renaissance, so the reconstruction, on a huge scale, of the Potsdamer Platz quarter reflects Berlin's ambitions to become the business capital of Germany.

The Potsdamer Platz was a pivotal space in pre-war Berlin, a hectic, dynamic, perhaps slightly seedy, focus for the Weimar capital. Its location, between the historic centre of government in the east and the growing commercial and residential belt to the west, was crucial – as was the coming of the railway from Potsdam. By the end of the 19th century, the station was the city's busiest and what had been the periphery of Berlin became its heart. Hotels, restaurants and big stores, including Eric Mendelsohn's magnificent Columbushaus, made the Potsdamer Platz a magnet for Berliners and outsiders, overshadowing the two elegant gatehouses designed in the early 19th century by Karl Friedrich Schinkel as part of a (failed) attempt to create a formal square – ironically, the success of the area owed a good deal to its essentially random and unplanned character, a riposte to Prussian (and Nazi) notions of order.

The old Potsdamer Platz was largely razed by wartime bombs (though the Columbushaus survived, in an increasingly poor state, into the 1950s). Its position, straddling the eastern and western zones, meant that it was still pivotal to the city, but the erection of the Wall saw the crossing point closed and the Potsdamer Platz became a forlorn wasteland. (The development, just over the Wall, of the Kulturforum, with its Mies van der Rohe National Gallery and concert hall and library by Hans Scharoun, served only to highlight the desolation.)

After the demolition of the Wall and the reunification of Germany, the reconstruction of the Potsdamer Platz became an issue – in terms of location and symbolism, the area was critical to the reconstruction of the city. A competition, launched by the city authorities in 1991, resulted in a masterplan by Hilmer & Sattler

top right
A plan showing the Potsdamer Platz scheme in relation to the centre of the city.

right
The Potsdamer Platz, located at a crucial hub between the governmental centre of Berlin in the east and the commercial heartland to the west, became the heart of the pre-1939 city, as shown in this contemporary photograph.

REICHSTAG
ALEXANDERPLATZ

WEINHAUS
RHEINGOLD

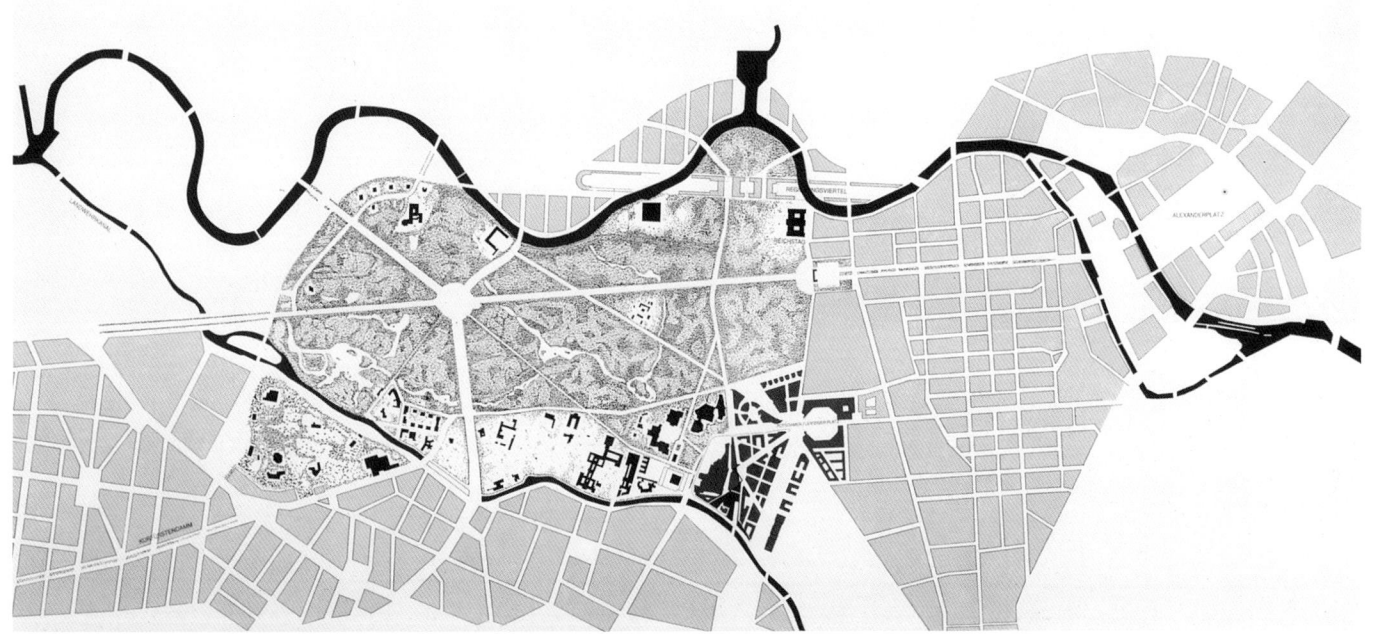

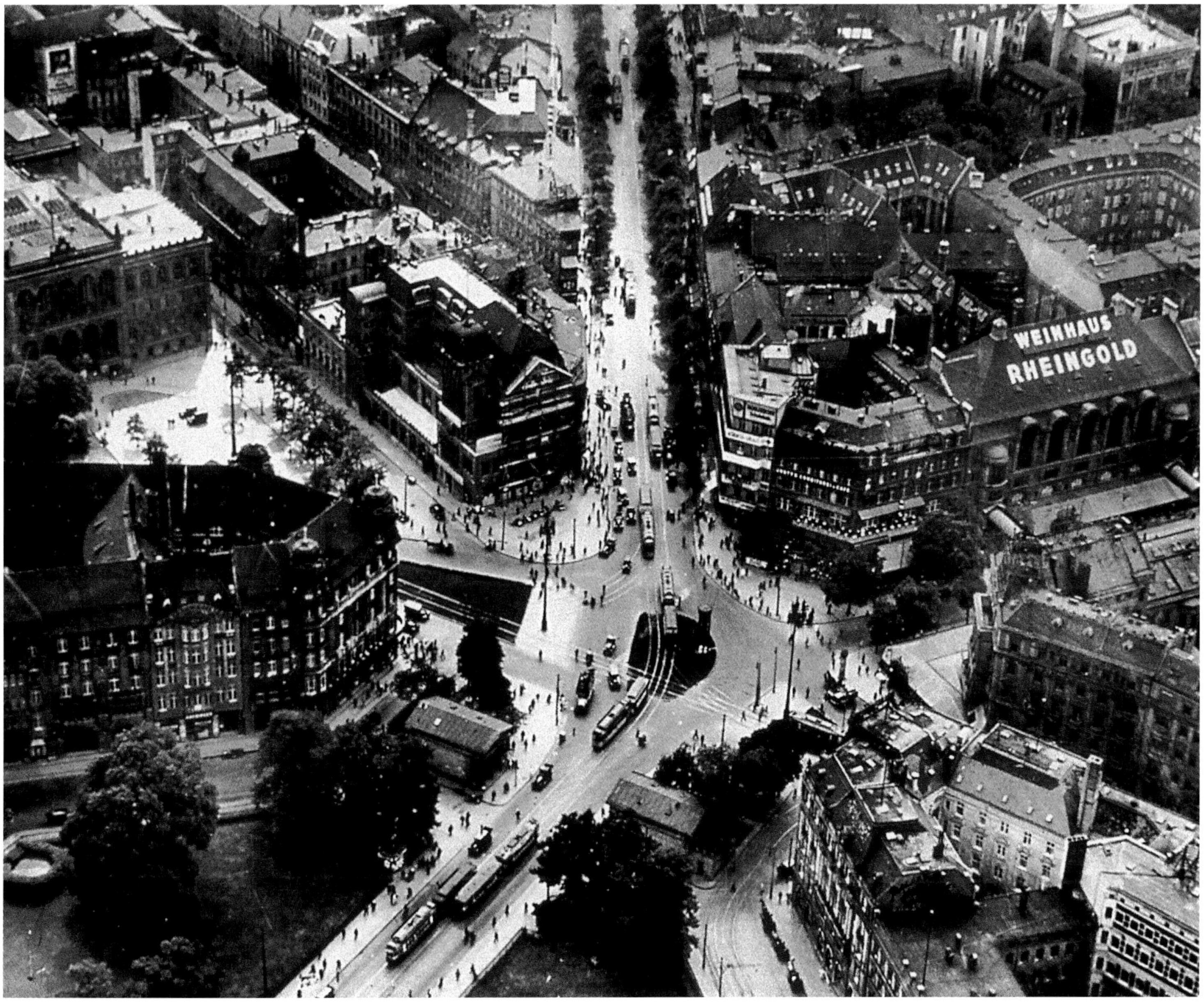

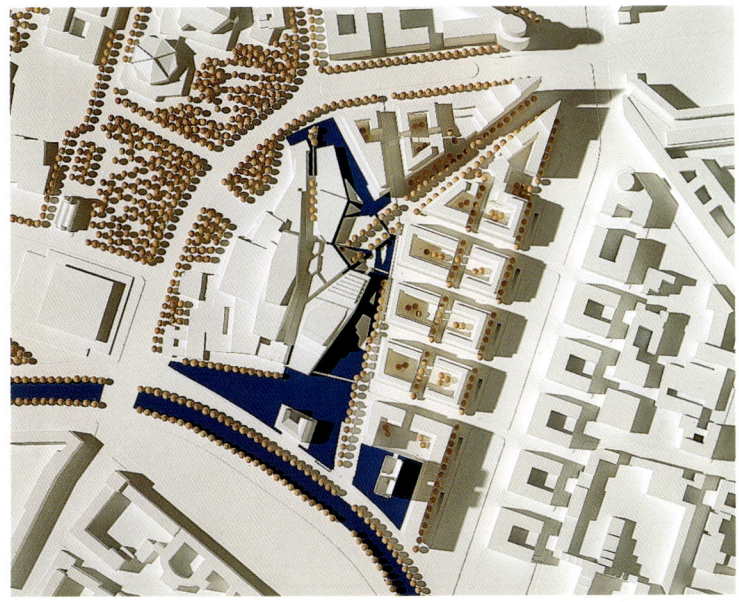

being selected over more radical proposals by Daniel Libeskind, Will Alsop and others. The masterplan proposed a series of blocks of strictly controlled dimensions, set along conventional streets – at last, Potsdamer Platz was to be given an orderly form (as Schinkel had intended). For some, the plan, in keeping with the overall philosophy of Berlin planning supremo Hans Stimman, reeked of authoritarianism – in a city where architecture and politics were intimately linked. Implementing it meant, however, in a free market economy, persuading land owners and developers of its merits, so that the way was open for a critical reassessment of the

left
Renzo Piano's 1992 masterplan has become the basis for the redevelopment of a huge swathe of the city left derelict since the Second World War.

above and right
Piano's plan is based, in response to guidelines laid down by the city, on the traditional city block. Large areas of office space are combined with residential, retail and leisure uses.

overleaf
Looking northeast down the covered Potsdamer Platz arcade with the IMAX theatre to the left.

office	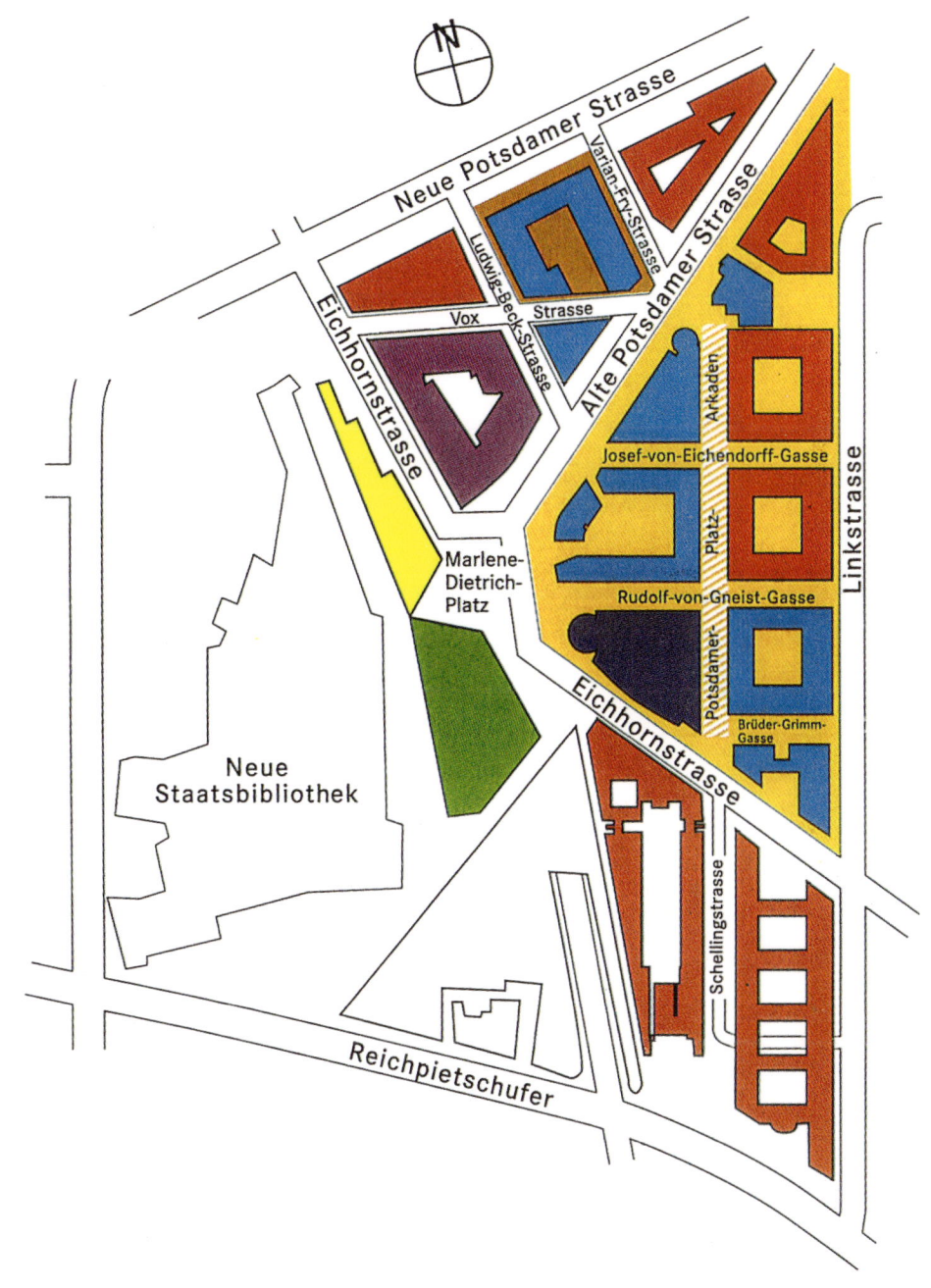
residential	
Hotel Grand Hyatt	
IMAX theatre	
musical theatre	
casino	
CINEMAXX centre	
retail	
Potsdamer Platz arcades	

above
With its use of
traditional materials
and strongly
articulated forms,
Piano's architecture
reinstates a sense of
civic order to an area
erased from the map by
wartime bombing.

right
Piano's Daimler Benz
tower is the tallest
building in the
development – its
terracotta cladding
is a concession to
local building
traditions. Opposite
it can be seen the
Haus Canaris, one
of the few old
buildings to remain
on the site.

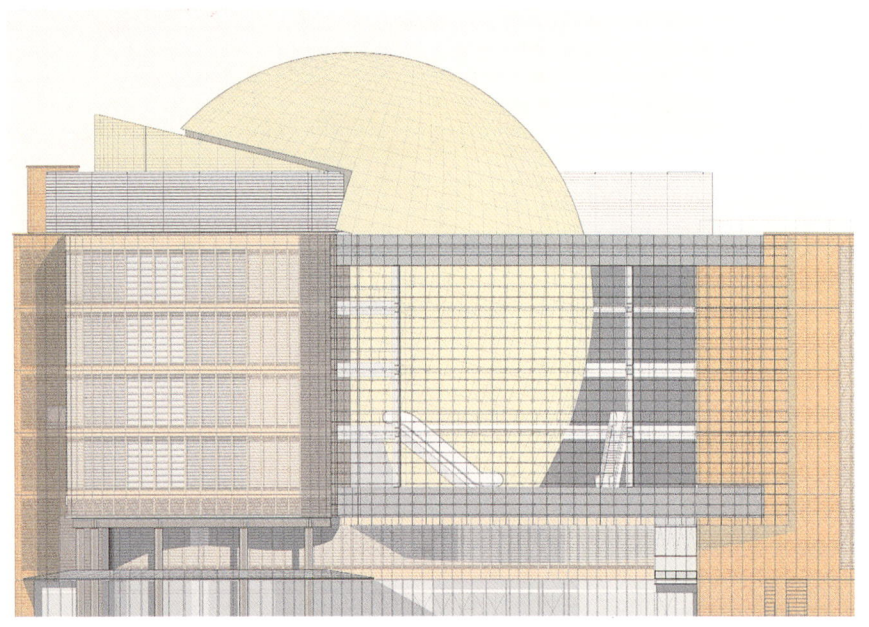

Piano and Kohlbecker's
IMAX cinema (left and
top left), hotel,
casino and musical
theatre (above)
around the Marlene
Dietrichplatz, at
the heart of the
development, reflect
the pre-1939 role of
the Potsdamer Platz
as a focus for
entertainment.

masterplan. Despite the rejection, by city planners, of a revised masterplan by Richard Rogers, done for Daimler Benz and including a striking tower overlooking the reconstructed square, enlightened commercialism has shaped the new quarter.

In 1992 Daimler Benz's development arm, debis, appointed Renzo Piano (with German architect Christoph Kohlbecker) to oversee the development of its site (totalling over 600,000 square metres/6.5 million square feet) at Potsdamer Platz. Working with an international design team (including Rogers), Piano has subtly subverted the original masterplan. While conceding that 'modernisation must not undermine the character of the city', he has created a dense and visually varied urban quarter which aims to balance public and private space. The reconstruction of the Friedrichstrasse, which was well under way before work started at Potsdamer Platz, suggested that strict adherence to traditional planning models did not make for a lively city. Perhaps it was his astute choice of materials, notably terracotta cladding, which allowed him to succeed where Rogers failed – the Daimler Benz HQ at the southern end of the development is, by Berlin standards, a skyscraper, breaking free of the discipline of the block. Other buildings conform more closely to the Stimman prototype, yet the brilliant device of linking them internally with a glazed retail mall – toplit, like the arcades of the 19th century and genuinely grand in scale – has created a vast public space at the heart of the site. Though critics have questioned the definition of this internal space as 'public', it is enormously popular with Berliners – 200,000 people came there on the opening day. More significant, perhaps, is the open air space of the Marlene Dietrich Platz, a really generous square with theatres, a casino, cinemas and a big hotel – a clear attempt to rekindle the spirit of Weimar Berlin. Within the Piano masterplan, there was scope for more than one aesthetic – the stolid rationalism of Rafael Moneo's blocks and the stodginess of the Volksbank building (by Arata Isozaki, with Steffen Lehmann) contrasts with the romantic lightness of Rogers (who is still clearly reluctant to be forced into an alien mould).

Piano's covered public spaces, a key element in the Potsdamer Platz project, draw on the 19th-century arcade tradition. The atrium of the Daimler Benz tower (right) is used for exhibitions and other events. The retail space which runs through the development (left) has become immensely popular with Berliners.

left
By using a team of architects for the design of the individual buildings, Piano has ensured a variety of form and materials within the discipline of the masterplan. The office and residential blocks on the Linkstrasse, designed by Richard Rogers Partnership, are strongly modelled, with some of the bravura of earlier High-tech projects by Rogers and Piano.

right
Much of the architecture of the new Potsdamer Platz is in the High-tech tradition, including the block by Richard Rogers Partnership.

North of the debis area is the big site developed by Sony, with Helmut Jahn as architect. If Piano subverted the Hilmer & Sattler plan, Jahn confronted it head on and appears to have largely bypassed it. The weakest aspect of the masterplan, Jahn believed, was that it was not spatial – 'a model for new urban activity and interaction, a new type of city space' was required. The Sony Centre includes Sony's own European headquarters, offices, apartments, the German Filmhaus, a multiplex cinema complex and large areas of leisure and retail use – nearly 158,000 square metres (1.7 million square feet) of space in total. The tensile-roofed Forum is the stunning centrepiece of the development – technically innovative, the great roof not only

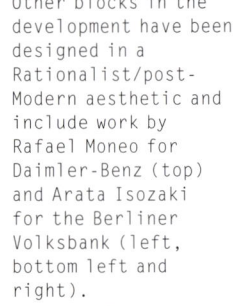

Other blocks in the development have been designed in a Rationalist/post-Modern aesthetic and include work by Rafael Moneo for Daimler-Benz (top) and Arata Isozaki for the Berliner Volksbank (left, bottom left and right).

Helmut Jahn's colossal (158,000 square metre/1.7 million square foot) Sony Center, which includes offices, apartments, shops, cinemas and other leisure facilities, is a brash and exuberant riposte to the discipline of the masterplan.

provides a big, weather-proof public space, eleven storeys high – it equally insulates surrounding buildings from the weather and provides energy economies. As in the much earlier State of Illinois Center in Chicago, Jahn provides offices which have views both outside and inside to a vast covered space. The Sony Centre is spectacular even by Jahn's standards, its exuberance – some would say brashness and even vulgarity – is set to outface Piano's more controlled blocks and overpower the subtler geometry of Scharoun's Philharmonie.

The overall success of the vast Potsdamer Platz project cannot yet be assessed, but it will rest on much more than mere letting figures and retail turnovers. Once the novelty of the new urban quarter, completed in time for the millennium, has worn off, it is its ability to relate to the rest of the city, to become a pivot and a meeting point of east and west, which will be the measure of its success.

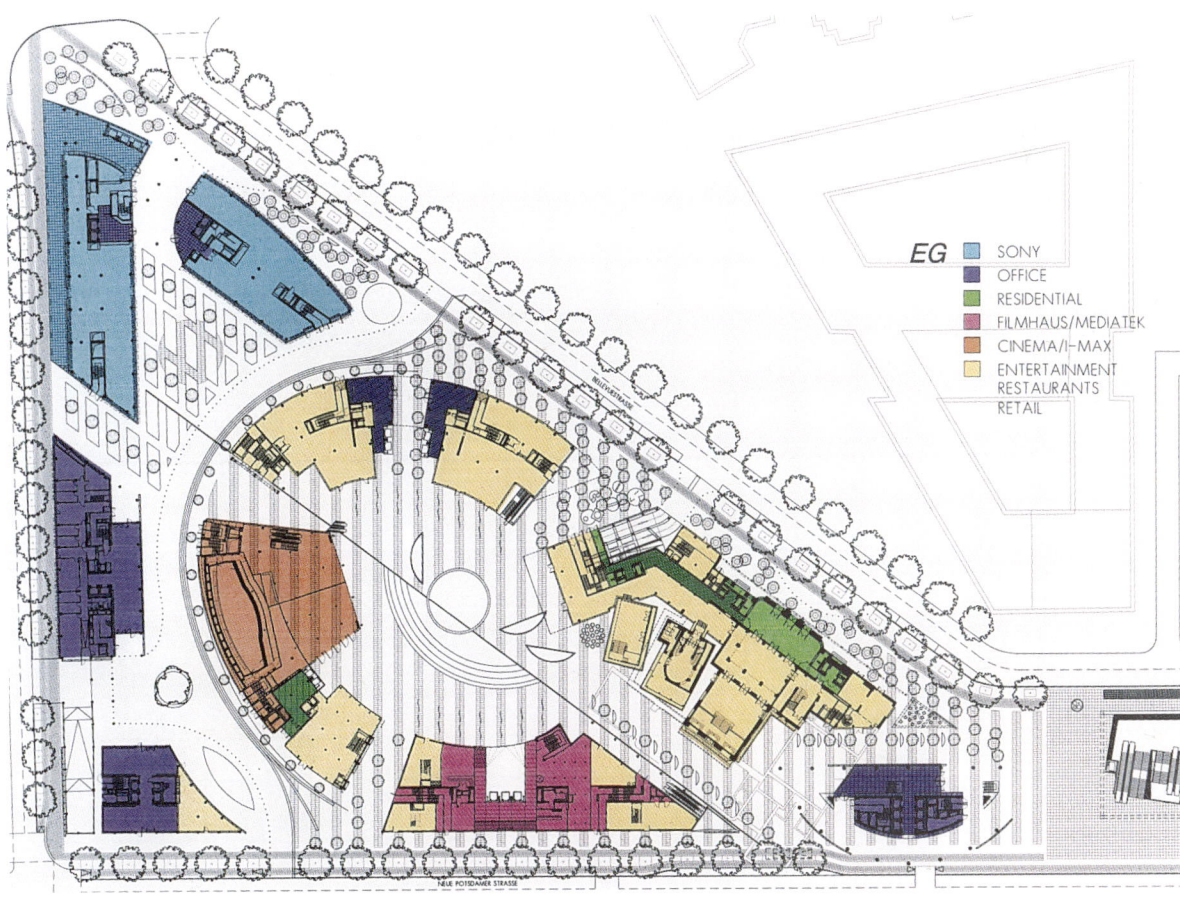

EG
- SONY
- OFFICE
- RESIDENTIAL
- FILMHAUS/MEDIATEK
- CINEMA/I-MAX
- ENTERTAINMENT
  RESTAURANTS
  RETAIL

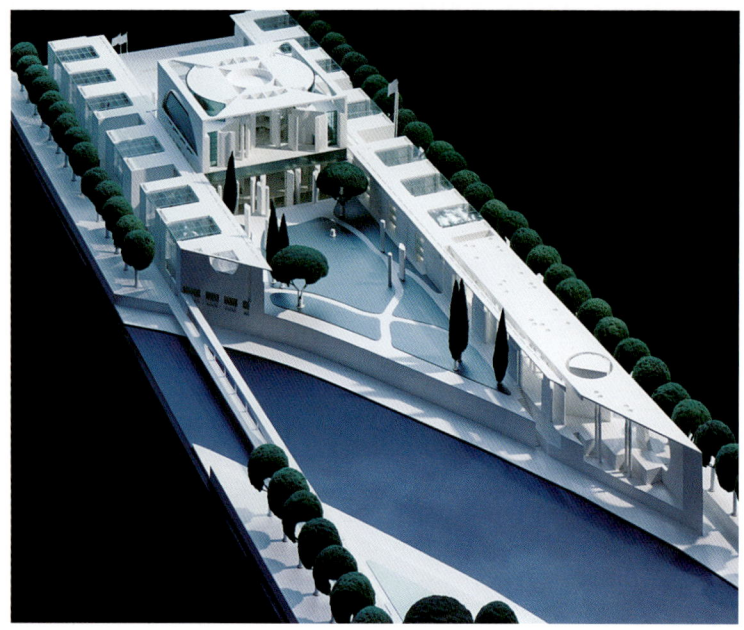

While Berlin's commercial regeneration was taking shape in the Potsdamer Platz, reconstruction of its government centre had begun just to the north. Charlotte Frank's masterplan for the Spreebogen quarter provides a ribbon of ministries and other government buildings which culminates in a new Federal Chancellery, thus imposing on Berlin a new character as a re-emerging political capital. The Spreebogen masterplan also gives a context to the Reichstag – the Kaiser's parliament and the seat of the 1919–33 Republic – which used to be the lone government building in the area. Norman Foster was commissioned to rebuild the historically important Reichstag. Foster's dome, which illuminates the debating chamber, has become not only an internal symbol of democratic transparency, but when seen from outside it also serves as a beacon to Berliners – a reminder of their city's new identity.

above and top left
Schultes' Federal Chancellery is the focal point of the 'ribbon' of government buildings straggling the great bend of the River Spree, close to the restored Reichstag building.

left
Charlotte Frank's masterplan for the Spreebogen quarter of Berlin – containing ministries and other federal buildings – was the competition winner in 1992.

right
The Reichstag building, restored by Norman Foster as the seat of the Federal Parliament, is one of the most striking of the Berlin *grands projets*.

right: top, bottom and centre
The masterplan developed by Group 91 Architects builds on the established strengths of the area, notably its wealth of historic buildings and well preserved street pattern, while seeking to create new public spaces and improved connections with the rest of the city.

below
The Temple Bar quarter lies on the south bank of the river Liffey, close to the historic heart of the Irish capital.

DUBLIN
Temple Bar

(1991–2000)

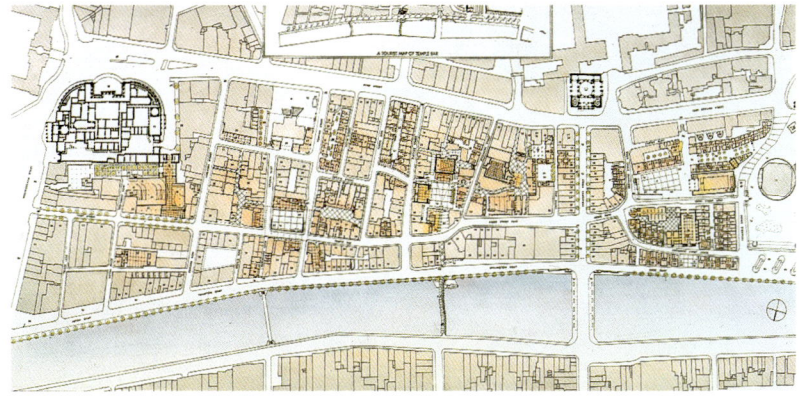

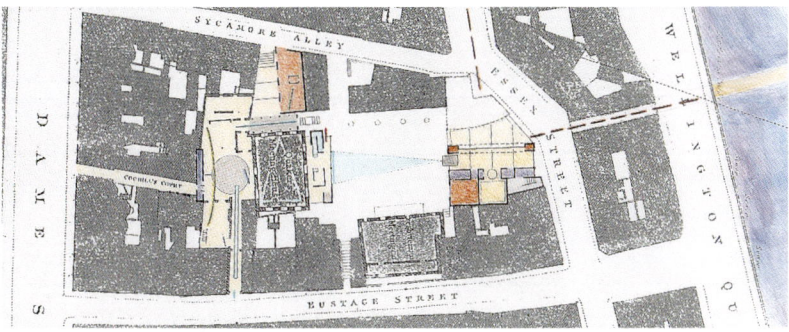

Though a small country and, in many respects, culturally conservative, Ireland was receptive to modern architecture from the early 1930s onwards. Dublin airport (completed 1941) and the city's bus station (1953) were major Modernist monuments. The bus station was the work of Michael Scott, whose distinguished practice, Scott Tallon Walker, achieved a number of significant works within the Irish capital as the Irish economy enjoyed its first major boom in the 1960s. Not all the new development of that period, however, was either distinguished or appropriate to its context in a great historic city – hundreds of Georgian buildings were thoughtlessly destroyed – and a vigorous conservationist backlash was the result, with modern design pilloried as a destructive force. Some of the battles of the 1960s and 1970s are now being re-staged, as it were, as Dublin experiences an even greater boom period at the beginning of the 21st century, though it is increasingly less likely that historic buildings and areas will be sacrificed to redevelopment.

The Temple Bar project demonstrates that new architecture and conservation can work together to produce enjoyable cities. Seen as a huge success in civic and commercial terms, Temple Bar has done much to recast the image of Dublin and underscore its new 'post-colonial' status as a European capital, proud of its past and eager to embrace the future, as well as reinforcing its attractions as a tourist destination. Most significantly, perhaps, it is the first major step towards bringing back the city centre's residential population, gradually decimated by the development policies of the last half century. (It had been halved, in fact, in less than 25 years.)

Temple Bar is an area of 14 hectares (35 acres) on the southern bank of the river Liffey, close to Trinity College, the Irish Parliament complex, Dublin's City Hall, and the ancient Christ Church Cathedral. As part of the 1960s strategy for redeveloping the city, the area was under sentence of death – to be flattened for a giant new transport interchange linked to a new metro line. Yet the vitality and diversity of the

left, bottom and far right
O'Donnell Tuomey's Irish Film Centre is a renovated eighteenth-century Quaker meeting house and occupies a key position at the heart of the area.

right
A model of the Irish Film Centre seen from above, highlighting its distinctive circular foyer.

area, 'Dublin's Marais', remained undimmed: indeed, its increasingly rundown character attracted new businesses and cultural ventures – small theatres, art galleries, recording studios – attracted by low rents, who took up buildings vacated by the traditional clothing industries of the area. At this period, 'cultural industries' were beginning to register as an important element in the Irish economy. The abandonment of the redevelopment project in 1987 led to a competition in 1991 aimed at securing a framework for renewal and regeneration. The competition, organised by the state-backed Temple Bar Properties Ltd, was won by the Group 91 consortium of eight Irish architectural practices.

The aims of the plan were repair and renewal – retaining and refurbishing the vast majority of surviving buildings and infilling a number of cleared sites with appropriate new structures. The mixed use pattern was to be

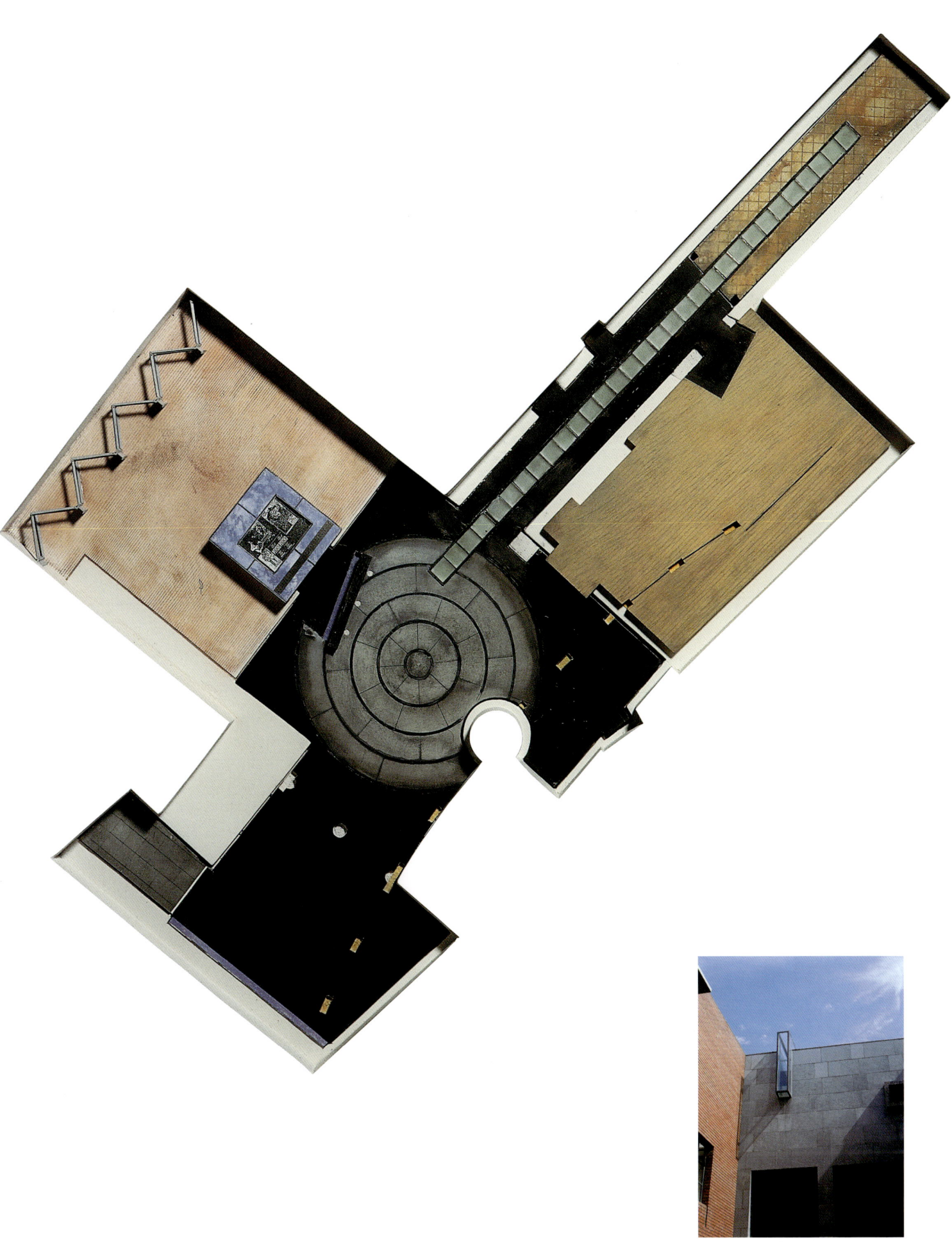

O'Donnell Tuomey's
National
Photographic
Archive is typical of
the new cultural
facilities developed
as a consequence of
the Temple Bar
project.

retained and reinforced, with a strong emphasis on nurturing cultural enterprises, including the expanding Irish film industry, more shops and restaurants catering for tourists and the local population, and an augmented residential population of around 3,000 people – a ten-fold increase. It is no accident that Derek Tynan, a prominent member of Group 91, had worked with Colin Rowe in the USA – Temple Bar is about applying the lessons of *Collage City*. Others in the group had worked for James Stirling and were influenced by the urban approach of Leon Krier and Aldo Rossi, a direct counter to the North American influences prevalent in the Dublin of the 1950s and 1960s.

Central to the plan is its stress on public space. While it seeks to retain the historic street pattern of Temple Bar, it also addresses the need to create better links to the rest of the city – the area had survived as a ghetto, but needed to be integrated to prosper in the future. A new bridge across the Liffey was considered a vital ingredient, but the proposal subsequently foundered after planning objections to the commissioned design. The existing east-west spine along Fleet Street to Essex Gate and Christ Church Cathedral has been supplemented by a new parallel route, more informal and clearly intended for pedestrians. A series of new squares has been created, again informal and un-monumental, gathering places for people – Temple Bar Square, Meeting House Square (with the new Irish Film Centre) and the adjacent Curved Street, with new cultural buildings on either side.

The ideals of integrated use and community development contained in the 1991 plan are reflected in The Printworks, a part refurb, part new-build mixed use scheme by Derek Tynan which is amongst the most successful of the new developments in Temple Bar which balances a strong street presence with the creation of a calm private world away from the crowds.

Temple Bar is, in many respects, a product of the post-Modern consciousness, yet its architectural expression returns frequently to

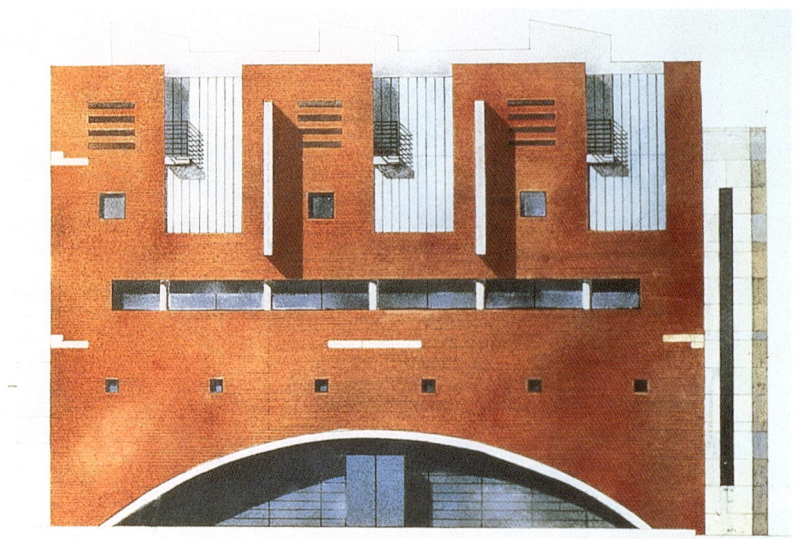

classic Modern Movement – specifically, Corbusian – sources. Elsewhere, for example in the National Photographic Archive building designed by O'Donnell & Tuomey, a Stirlingesque Rational-Classical aesthetic predominates. Materials generally are street-friendly, with lavish use of brick and render. Where appropriate, as in the case of Burke-Kennedy Doyle's Spranger's Yard housing, the overriding aim seems to be to defer to historic context. There is a strong case for some 'background architecture' of this sort in Temple Bar, but some of the more recent housing proposals put forward by commercial developers seem to fall short of the promise contained in the plan.

Equally in doubt is the viability of creating a mixed-income community – many apartments are used as *pieds-à-terre* by Dublin professionals – and of preserving enterprises which depend on cheap rents in an area which has become a lucrative tourist honeypot after the model of London's Covent Garden (where the same questions arise). Architects cannot exercise economic and social hegemony. Yet the degree of integration between architecture and urban design achieved at Temple Bar is remarkable and should ensure that the quarter has the potential for change and self-renewal that will make it a vital part of Dublin for centuries to come.

left
The architecture of O'Donnell Tuomey's Meeting House Square is contextual, in a broadly Rationalist tradition.

right and below
The new Poddle footbridge across the Liffey, designed by McGarry NiEanaigh Architects, was considered a vital element of the masterplan, but has yet to be realized.

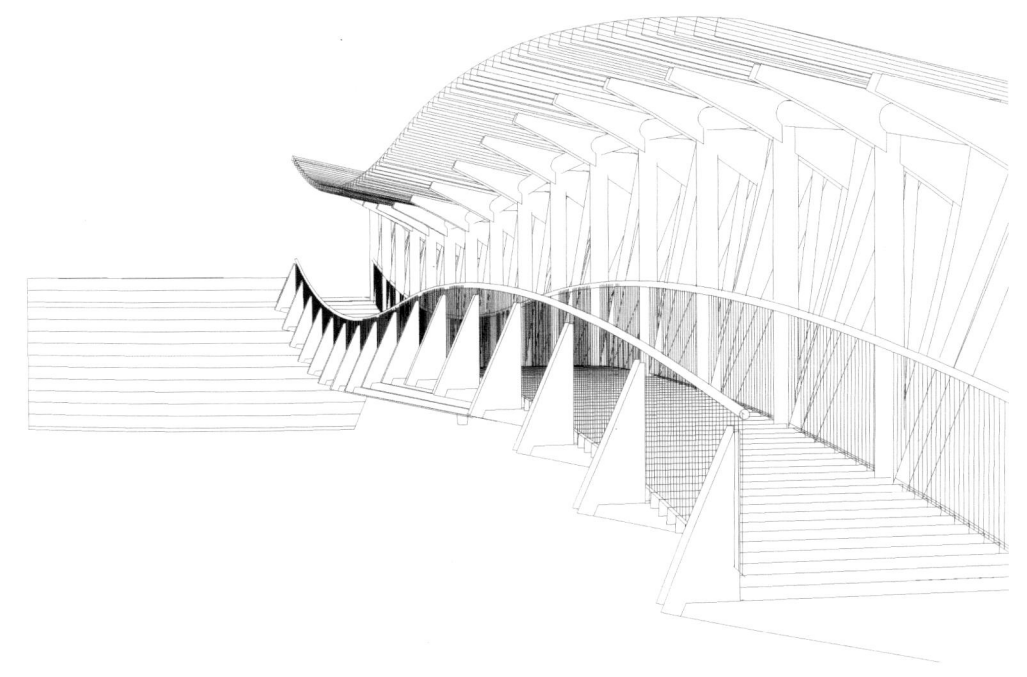

Genoa's celebration in 1992 of the 500th anniversary of Columbus's Atlantic voyage launched a regeneration project for the city's historic port district.

GENOA
Columbus International Exhibition and renewal of the old port

(1988–2000)

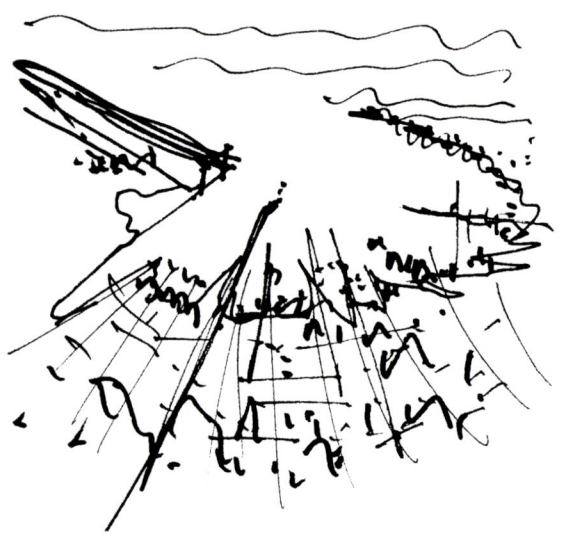

Genoa is one of the great historic cities of Italy and has been one of the key ports of the Mediterranean since the Middle Ages. Unlike its erstwhile rival, Venice, however, Genoa has remained a major commercial centre into the present century and its ancient streets, churches and palazzi are balanced by large scale 19th- and 20th-century developments. Genoa is a dynamic centre of business, education and the arts and the capital of the Ligurian region. Beyond the historic core, heavy industries, including steel, shipbuilding and chemicals, developed along the coast, beyond the international airport (opened in 1962). The port itself has spread steadily outwards from the ancient quays close to the city centre with well-connected container terminals. It is still a major employer and a foundation of the regional economy, but is increasingly detached from the life of the city. The old streets close to the Molo are unchanged after many centuries, but the area has long suffered from physical and social decay, its survival until recently in some doubt.

Renzo Piano Building Workshop, a world famous practice based in Genoa (where Piano was born), was first approached in 1984 to develop ideas for the 500th anniversary, in 1992, of Christopher Columbus's Atlantic voyage. Piano – who had previously worked on a regeneration project for the Quartiere del Molo – identified the old port area as the inevitable location for the celebrations, which could be used as the launching-point for a much-needed process of regeneration extending into the 21st century. Developing tourism was one objective – it was ironic that the quays, from which Genoa's importance derived, were inaccessible to visitors. (The isolation of the old port had been symbolically reinforced by the demolition of buildings and the construction of the *strada sopraelevata* along the dock front in the 1960s – though the barrier was more psychological than physical.) But Piano argued also that the old port was a potential amenity for the city's commercial and cultural life – Genoa badly needed a convention and exhibition centre, for example.

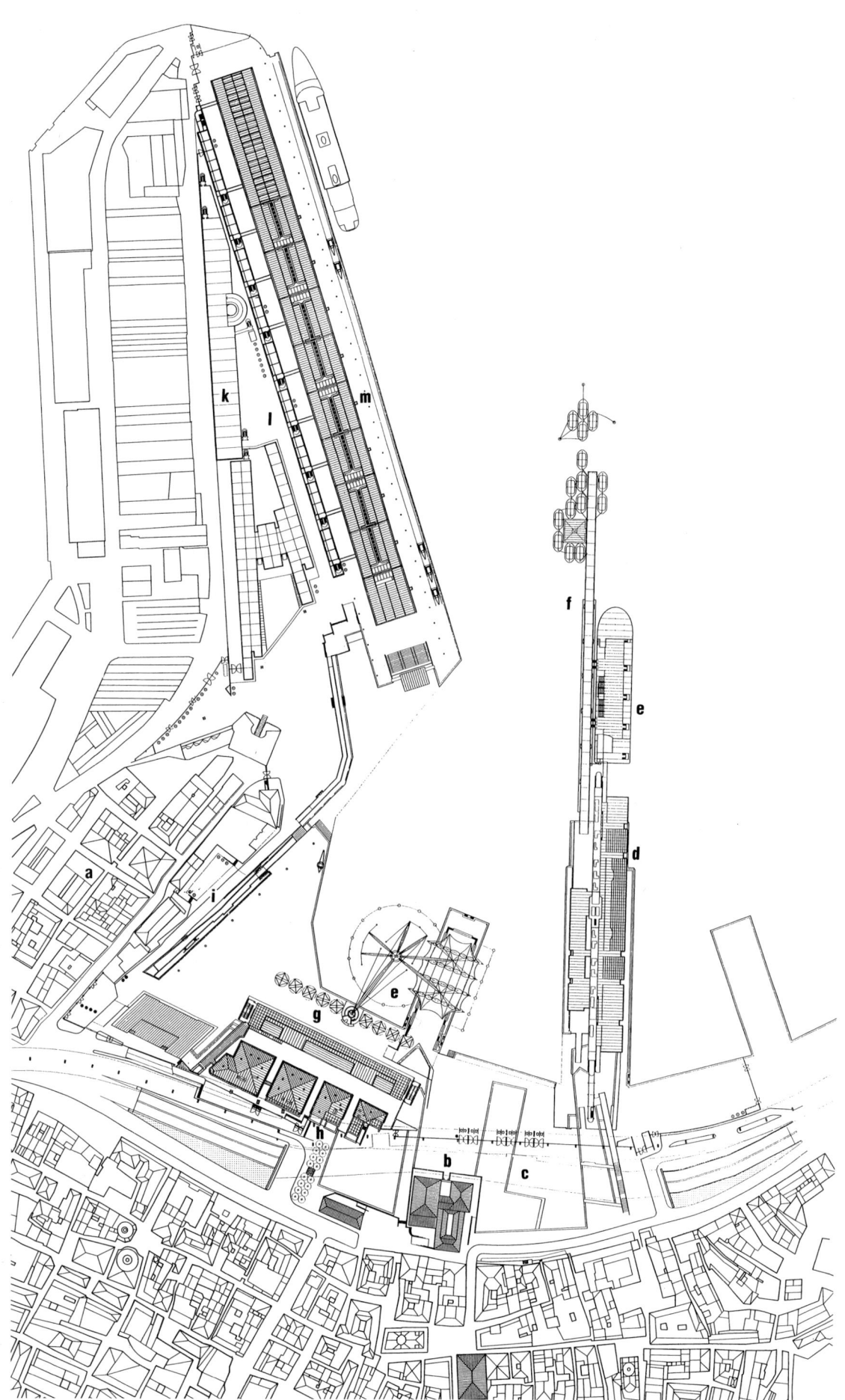

left
The masterplan
focussed on an area of
the old port close to
the ancient heart of
Genoa but long closed
to outsiders - the
city had previously
been cut off from the
Mediterranean.

right
Details of the sail-
like canopies
connected to the Bigo
at the port's centre,
continuing Piano's
maritime theme.

Piano wanted to show 'the real face' of Genoa to the world. His strategy involved a typically late 20th-century mix of striking new architecture and renovation. The largest asset in the area was the tremendous run of 1900s cotton warehouses extending along the dock and built, to the design of British engineers, to a very high specification. These buildings, long disused, were retained intact and converted as exhibition spaces, with a later addition completely rebuilt behind the facades to create a 1,500-seat conference hall. The need for selective demolition was clear and a further building was reduced by the removal of (relatively recent) upper floors to create a panoramic terrace and restaurant.

Every regeneration area needs a landmark, a signature building which identifies it. Piano's 'Bigo' – or derrick – seems, at first glance, something of an extravagant gesture. This enormous steel structure supports nothing more than a lift, whisking visitors upwards to enjoy a terrific view of the sea and city Yet the costly gesture has paid off – the Bigo points people to the renewed port quarter.

Along the Ponte Spinola quay a group of new buildings in a recognizably high-tech mould was constructed. The largest element here is the aquarium, located in what was one of the 1992 exhibition pavilions and extended, appropriately, into a floating section – virtually a ship.

The success of the Old Port regeneration has encouraged investment in the adjacent area of the city and streets which once seemed doomed to permanent decay are being gradually upgraded. Genoa's rediscovery of its ancient heart has paid off.

Piano's Bigo is unashamedly a landmark, designed as a symbol of regeneration and change, but draws on the historic imagery of derricks and cranes.

New buildings on the site include a major aquarium (left), housing (top right) and local government offices (bottom right).

KOBE
Hyogo Prefectural
Museum and
Waterfront plaza;
Rokko housing

(1997-2003)

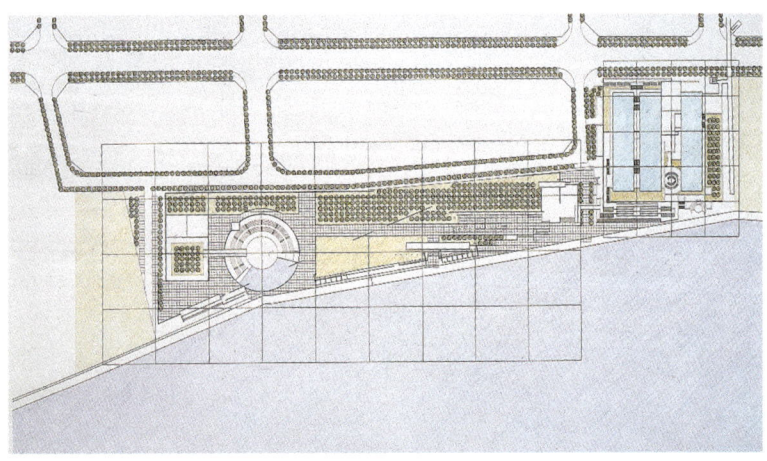

Like the great Lisbon earthquake of 1755, that which struck the Japanese port city of Kobe on 17 January, 1995, was not only a catastrophe in human and environmental terms but also the beginning of a new era. The post-earthquake reconstruction of Kobe has reflected the city's self confidence and optimism and its commitment to progressive urban ideals.

Over 5,000 people died in the 1995 disaster. Nearly 300,000 people were left homeless and some 50,000 buildings suffered significant damage. Within three years, however, Kobe's mayor, Kazutoshi Sasayama, was able to claim '80 per cent recovery'. This process involved not simply the repair of the damaged urban fabric, but dramatic moves to expand and enhance the city. Since the opening of its modern port in 1868, Kobe has been a go-ahead, cosmopolitan city, with an identity of its own (despite its proximity to the Osaka metropolis). The ongoing development of Port Island, with deep water berths for the largest container ships, is linked to the growth of new industries – Kobe was formerly heavily dependent on steel making. New road systems, including the Akashi Straits Bridge (opened in 1998), the new convention centre and the proposed expansion of Kobe's airport are all part of the same movement forward.

So too is Tadao Ando's new Hyogo Prefectural Museum of Modern Art, the centrepiece of a bold redevelopment of the waterfront east of the city centre – a zone formerly given over to now-defunct heavy industries. The building supplants the 1970s Hyogo Museum (designed by Togo Murano for another site). An open competition was held in 1997 and Ando's proposal was selected. Ando had already been commissioned by the city to design the new Waterfront Plaza, so that the two projects became interconnected. The new museum sits on a base of rock, which supports three glazed containers – Ando sees the contrast as a symbol of the new Kobe rising from the ruins of the old and the building as a memorial to the victims of the earthquake. The concentric plaza is designed as a place for events, but also

above
The museum itself comprises three glass boxes on a rock base.

right
The museum gardens include a circular plaza intended both for events and for quiet reflection.

left
Ando's Hyogo Prefectural Museum is the centrepiece of a redevelopment project for the former industrial area on the waterfront east of central Kobe. Set in a formal landscape, the museum is seen as a memorial to victims of the disastrous 1995 earthquake.

includes an area of woodland, a place for
reflection and remembrance.

Ando's Kobe housing project – begun as
early as 1981 and with a third phase due for
completion in 2003 – sits at the foot of the
Rokko mountains, overlooking Osaka Bay. Many
such sites in Japan have been ruthlessly
overdeveloped, with houses in regimented
ranks, set on stepped platforms. Ando's project
works with the steeply sloping site to create
views out to the ocean and into internal
gardens. The asymmetry of the scheme mirrors
the irregularities of the site. By including
community facilities – a swimming pool,
kindergarten and old people's day centre – in
the development, Ando has reasserted what he
calls 'the wonderful notion of congregation and
living together in harmony'. In essence, he is
creating a new city district with a life of its
own, a counterblast to the suburbanization of
modern Japan.

below and right
Tadao Ando's Rokko
housing project in
Kobe forms a new city
district, designed in
sympathy with the
dramatic contours of
the site.

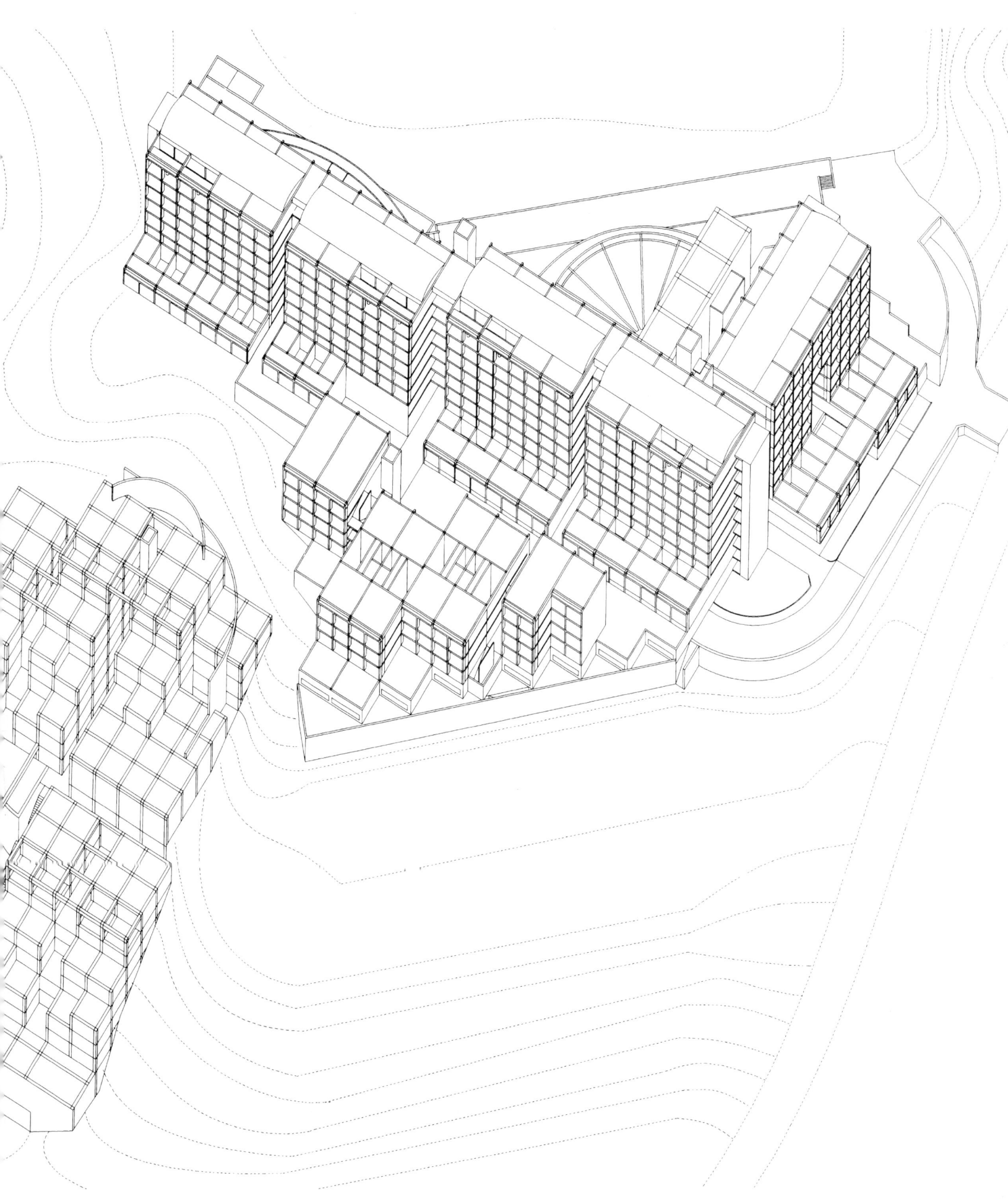

left
Dense and entirely
urban in character,
the Rokko housing
development – the first
phase dates from 1981
– steps down to the
waters of Osaka Bay.

below
Roof gardens take
advantage of fine
views of the ocean
and mountains.

LISBON
Reconstruction of
the Chiado
district

(1988-2000)

Alvaro Siza's
masterplan for the
fire-devastated
Chiado quarter of
Lisbon was founded on
an affection for an
area regarded as the
'soul' of the city.

Natural disasters have been a less frequent cause of urban change over the centuries than warfare or economic change, but modern Lisbon has its origins in the disastrous earthquake of 1755 which razed to the ground up to two thirds of the city. The great fire that swept the historic Chiado quarter, at the heart of the Portuguese capital in 1988 was, by comparison, limited in extent, but the significance of the area, famous, like Paris's Montmartre, for its associations with artists and writers and regarded as the 'soul' of Lisbon, made reconstruction imperative. The reconstruction project was awarded to Alvaro Siza and was probably instrumental in confirming Siza's standing as the most eminent living Portuguese architect – most of Siza's previous work had been in other countries.

The Chiado may have been the heart of the Old City of Lisbon, but prior to 1988 it was clearly in decline, 'strangled by nostalgia' as Siza put it. Though physically intact, its fabric mostly of 18th-century vintage, the area was suffering from a steady dwindling of the resident population and the commercial decline of the big turn-of-the-century stores that dominated the local retail trade – the Chiado was becoming shabby and seedy, with fast-food outlets the only growth point, and fashionable Lisbon had moved elsewhere. The fire, though apparently a catastrophe (four entire blocks and 18 historic buildings were wholly or partly destroyed), was actually the key to the future, opening the way for radical urban surgery.

Once surviving facades had been stabilized – and some, deemed unsafe, demolished – Siza began an intensive programme of research and analysis as the basis of a masterplan. Siza rejected the idea that the choice lay between restoration or new-build. He accepted that the old character of the area had to be retained (or re-created) – the scale of the buildings and the street pattern were sacrosanct. Architectural style was not an issue – what mattered was the creation of an urban pattern which would work well for present-day and future needs. The character of the city blocks was a critical issue: they needed to be opened up and made more

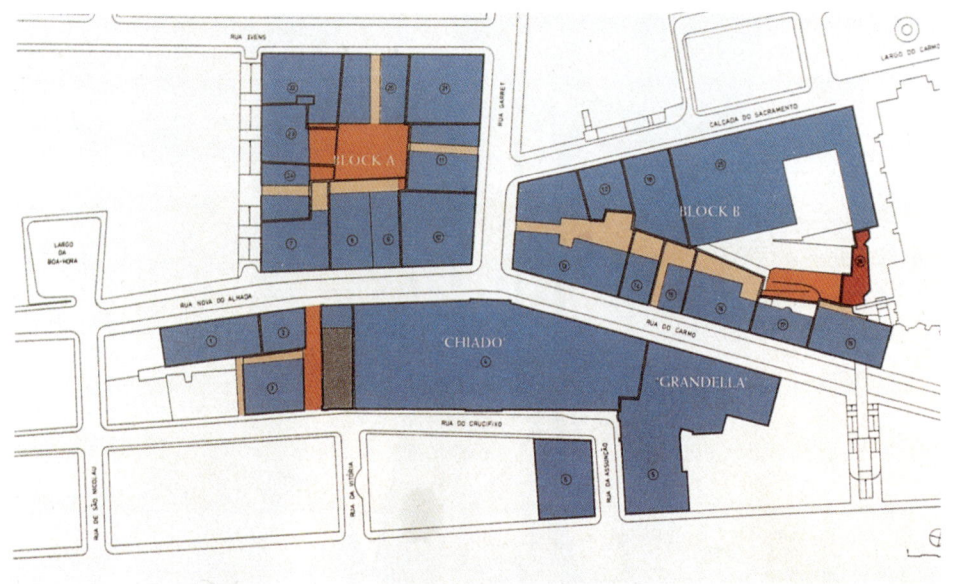

left and below
The Chiado project exploited the opportunities created by the fire to open up under-used backlands, developing behind restored historic frontages, to increase the area's resident population.

right
Newly built frontages such as this example are surprisingly undemonstrative in their simplicity.

RUA NOVA DO ALMADA

RUA GARRETT

RUA DO CARMO

above
A sectional view of
two streets as they
were before the fire.

left and right
The Camara Chaves
apartment building
demonstrates the
project's emphasis
on the retention of
historic facades
where possible,
as well as its
commitment to mixed-
use development.

permeable, so that residential use could be intensified (by at least 30 per cent) and through-routes established to integrate the Chiado into the fabric of the city – in view of the contours of the site, these include steps, ramps and lifts which link downtown Lisbon with the hilltop Bairro Alto quarter. The reconstruction of the local metro station, with much improved access, was another vital ingredient of the masterplan.

Those familiar with Siza's landmark projects – such as the Contemporary Art Museum in Santiago de Compostela – may find the undemonstrative nature of the new frontages in the Chiado surprising. But Siza insists that realities count for more than appearances, activity is the issue, not aesthetics. Behind the facades, radical reconstruction has taken place – most distinctively in those buildings, like the former Grandella store, a 1900s pile by the French architect Georges Demay, where Siza's office has designed the fit-out. Only at roof level does inventiveness surface externally.

Ten years after the fire, the rebuilding of the Chiado was far from complete and the project overlapped with the run-up to the 1998 Lisbon Expo, where Siza again assumed the masterplanning role (for a 60-hectare/148-acre site to the east of the city along the banks of the river Tagus) and also designed Portugal's national pavilion. The Expo was a celebration of Lisbon's pride of place and confidence in the future. Served by the new Oriente station (designed by Santiago Calatrava) the site has now been established as a new quarter of the capital. But Lisbon has also been careful to ensure the vitality of its historic core. At the Chiado, Siza has placed an understanding of geography and history at the centre of the urban agenda, merging conservation and new design to produce a really liveable city district.

Santiago Calatrava's new Oriente metro station was designed as part of a new quarter to serve Lisbon's Expo, also masterplanned by Siza.

Extending the City

The 19th century saw cities grow at a phenomenal rate and often with results that were disastrous for city dwellers: poor housing, overcrowding, industrial pollution, disease and sheer ugliness. The ill effects of unplanned growth fuelled the demand for planned cities, zoning and all the ills which, in turn, came out of the rejection of laissez-faire. Yet there was always a middle way between uncontrolled sprawl and rigid control. Cerda's great plan for the expansion of Barcelona at the end of the 19th century demonstrated that it was possible to develop a framework which, while providing the basis for healthy city life, still allowed scope for individuality and for architectural invention. By the 1900s, Barcelona was notable both for the success of its masterplan and for the idiosyncratic and far from over-disciplined work of architects like Antoni Gaudí and Luis Domenech i Montaner. Such is the strength of the Barcelona grid that it has remained the flexible foundation for the growth of the city into the 21st century.

For most major western cities, the obvious points for future growth are the derelict areas left vacant by the demise of old industries, including traditional docklands. Manhattan was ringed by wharves and piers where passengers and freight arrived close to the heart of New York. Air travel and new freight handling techniques made these facilities redundant. Part of the character of New York was lost, yet there was also the opportunity to break down the walls and extend the city down to the water. South Seaport is in the Quincy Market (Boston) tradition of retail-fed revival, attractive to tourists yet with little impact on the city as a whole. Battery Park City at the southern tip of Manhattan is vastly more ambitious, a true extension of the city, with the street and sidewalk, apartment block and corner deli, defining a familiar urban character. At the end of the 20th century, New York was turning its focus on the west side, using transport renewal as a catalyst to open up the wastes.

London's Canary Wharf took its cue, to some degree, from New York (where its developers were responsible for the office element of Battery Park City). Yet Canary Wharf was purely an office city - only in the late 1990s did its residential component finally begin to come on stream. The development was half-strangled at birth because of the absence of infrastructure - only when an efficient public transport link was promised did its success become assured. The approach at Rotterdam, where

the Kop van Zuid project has the potential to become Europe's
most successful dockland regeneration scheme, was very
different - new road and metro links were priorities.
At Duisburg's Inner Harbour - the largest inland expanse of
water in Europe - a similar strategy has marked the well-paced
development of Norman Foster's masterplan. The essence of these
projects is their aim to achieve real civility - the mix of uses
and income groups that characterizes the traditional city.
Yet it would be wrong to depict these projects as conservative
or retrograde. There is a dynamism to them, found equally
in Rem Koolhaas's masterplan for the city centre of Almere
- sometimes described as a late 20th-century garden city,
but set to acquire a real heart with the intensity of older
urban centres.

The growth of cities outside Europe is taking place at such
a frantic pace that attempts to constrain or direct their
expansion sometimes seem doomed to failure. Richard Rogers'
masterplan (1992-4) for the Lu Jia Zui quarter of Shanghai,
across the Huang Pu river from the old city centre and the
great commercial district of the Bund, has been largely
sidelined in the rush to develop the city - as have those drawn
up by Dominique Perrault, Toyo Ito, and Massimiliano Fuksas.
Shanghai wants (and is getting) an unbalanced clump of tall
office towers, an instant city modelled on North American
exemplars. It remains to be seen whether the high ideals
instilled by Kisho Kurokawa into his masterplan for Kuala
Lumpur's new airport can survive the enormous pressure to
secure growth at all costs.

HO CHI MINH CITY
Saigon South
Masterplan

(1993–2030)

Nothing could better illustrate the ongoing transformation of Vietnam into a potentially front-rank Asian capitalist economy than the masterplan created by the San Francisco office of Skidmore, Owings & Merrill to develop a vast (3300-hectare/8,000- acre) area to the south of the existing core of Ho Chi Minh City (HCMC) – formerly Saigon – as Saigon South, with new industries, office districts and residential areas, with a population of one million.

Saigon is not an ancient city. In the 18th century it was little more than a village, but it grew as a colonial trading centre under French rule during the 19th century and by 1939 had a population of around 500,000 – today it has over seven million inhabitants. The Doi Canal formed a natural boundary to the city to the south, separating the built-up area from the paddy fields and marshes beyond. To the east, the city's growth was constrained by the Saigon river.

With the tragic interlude of the Vietnam War over, the country looked to overseas investment to develop its still largely agrarian economy – the typical annual income of a Vietnamese in 1996 was only $300. The authorities of HCMC resolved to adopt a planned approach to future urban development and formed a partnership with Taiwan-based Central Trading and Development Group, which had already invested in the development of the city's port. SOM was appointed as masterplanner for the Saigon South project in 1993, working with Koetter Kim and Kenzo Tange Associates.

The impetus to the development of the south side of the city came from transport improvements, notably a new highway serving the airport and extending south of the Doi Canal. This is extended as the Saigon South Parkway to serve the city's new quarter.

Extending HCMC is seen as a way of making it not just a dynamic city, but also protecting its character and 'liveability' – further increases in the density of the old city can only result in the overdevelopment and pollution seen in Bangkok, Singapore and other

right
The SOM masterplan for Saigon South draws on the topography and ecology of the area to create a vast new extension of the city on the site of paddy fields and marshes (shown in the centre photograph). The Doi Canal formerly marked the edge of the city.

overleaf
The Saigon South masterplan provides an exceptionally bold and confident vision of a new city quarter, both urban in character and yet integrated with the natural landscape – an antidote to the uncontrolled sprawl of many Asian cities.

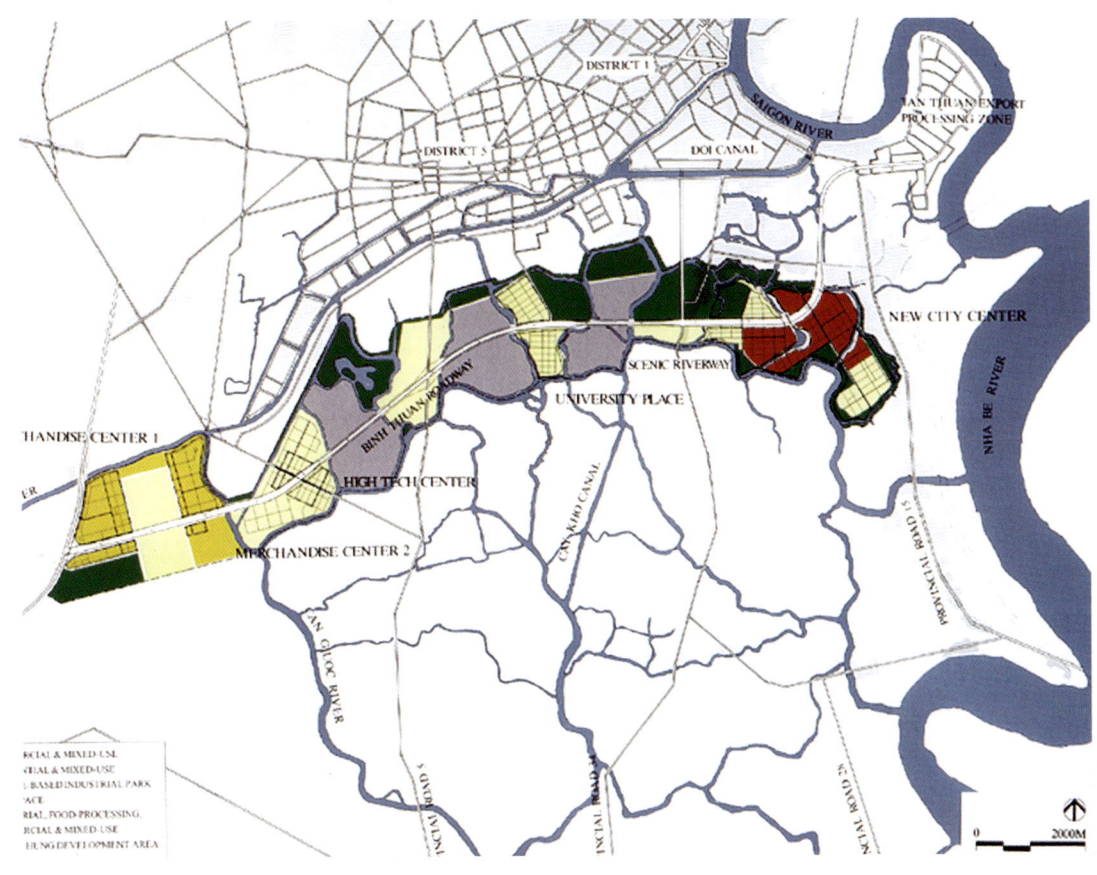

Legend (partial):
- RCIAL & MIXED-USE
- CIAL & MIXED-USE
- BASED INDUSTRIAL PARK
- ACE
- RIAL, FOOD-PROCESSING
- RCIAL & MIXED-USE
- HING DEVELOPMENT AREA

Map labels: DISTRICT 1, DISTRICT 5, SAIGON RIVER, DOI CANAL, TAN THUAN EXPORT PROCESSING ZONE, NEW CITY CENTER, NHA BE RIVER, SCENIC RIVERWAY, UNIVERSITY PLACE, BINH THUAN ROADWAY, HIGH TECH CENTER, HANDISE CENTER 1, MERCHANDISE CENTER 2

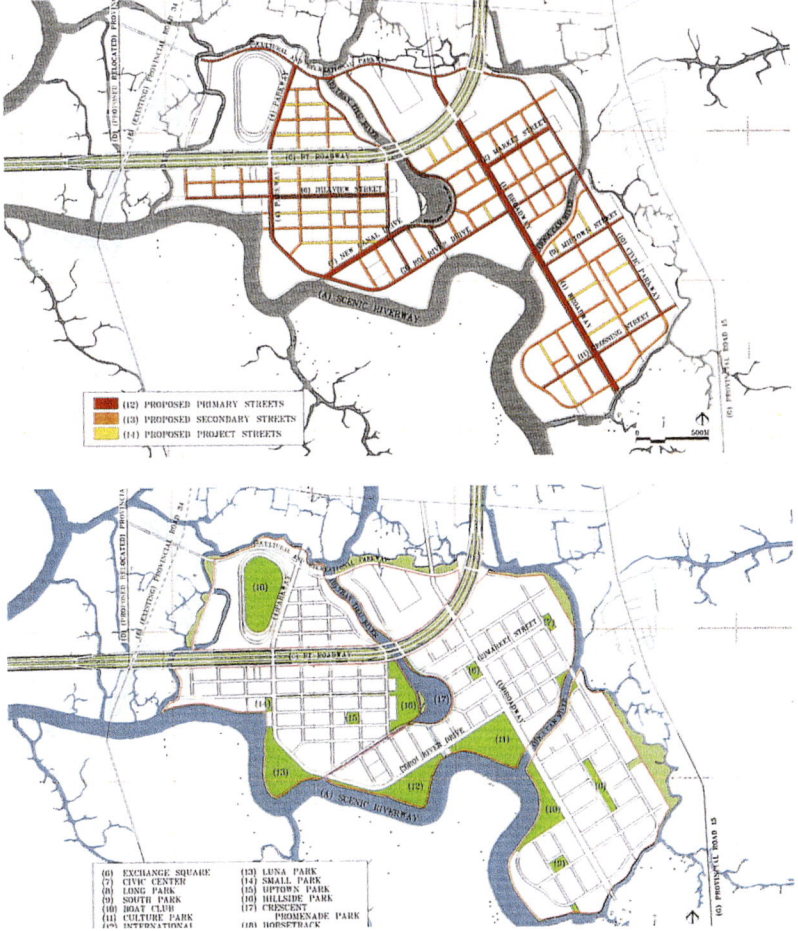

Legend:
- (12) PROPOSED PRIMARY STREETS
- (13) PROPOSED SECONDARY STREETS
- (14) PROPOSED PROJECT STREETS

Legend:
(6) EXCHANGE SQUARE	(13) LUNA PARK
(7) CIVIC CENTER	(14) SMALL PARK
(8) LONG PARK	(15) UPTOWN PARK
(9) SOUTH PARK	(16) HILLSIDE PARK
(10) BOAT CLUB	(17) CRESCENT
(11) CULTURE PARK	PROMENADE PARK
(12) INTERNATIONAL	(18) HORSETRACK

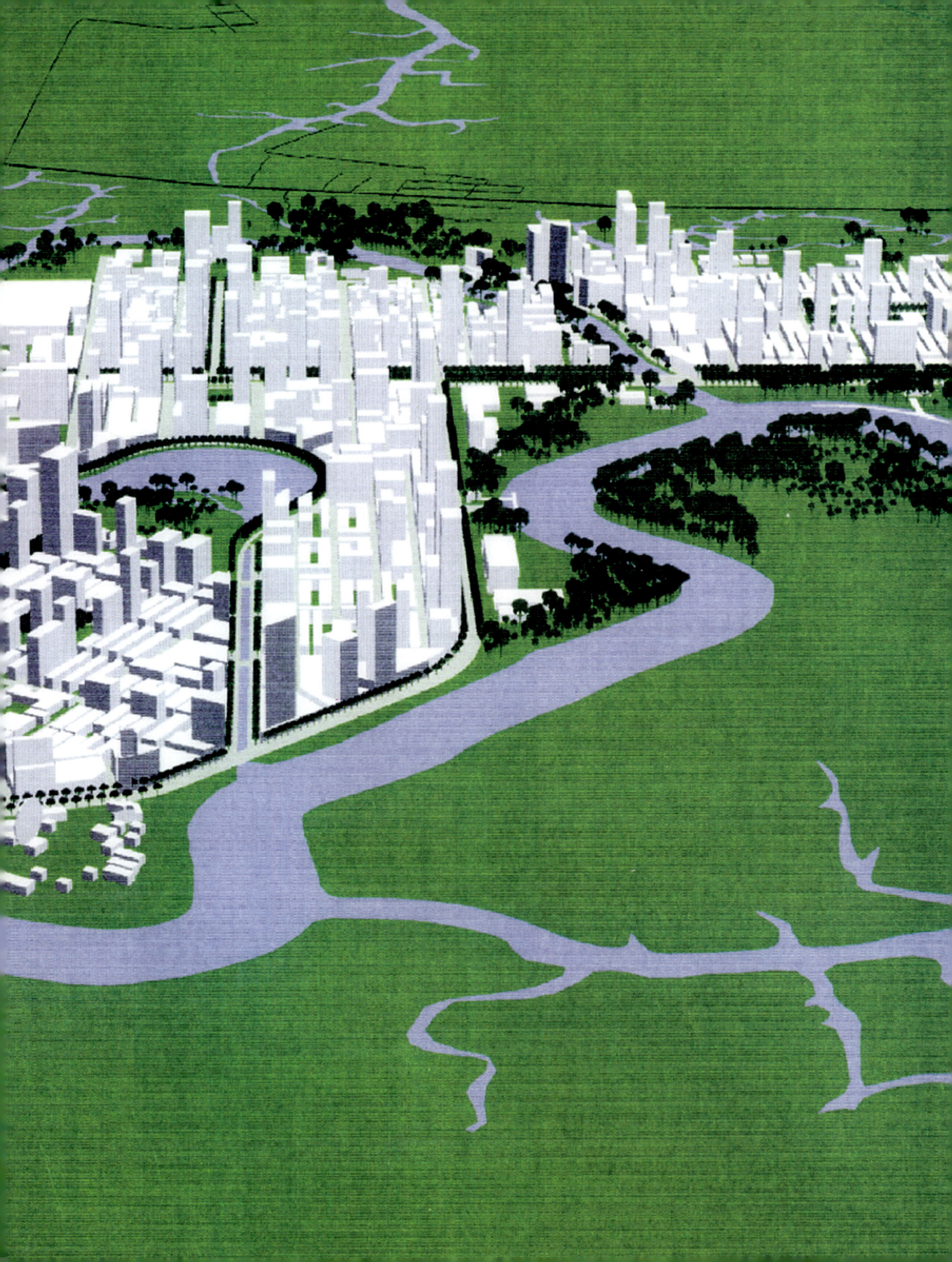

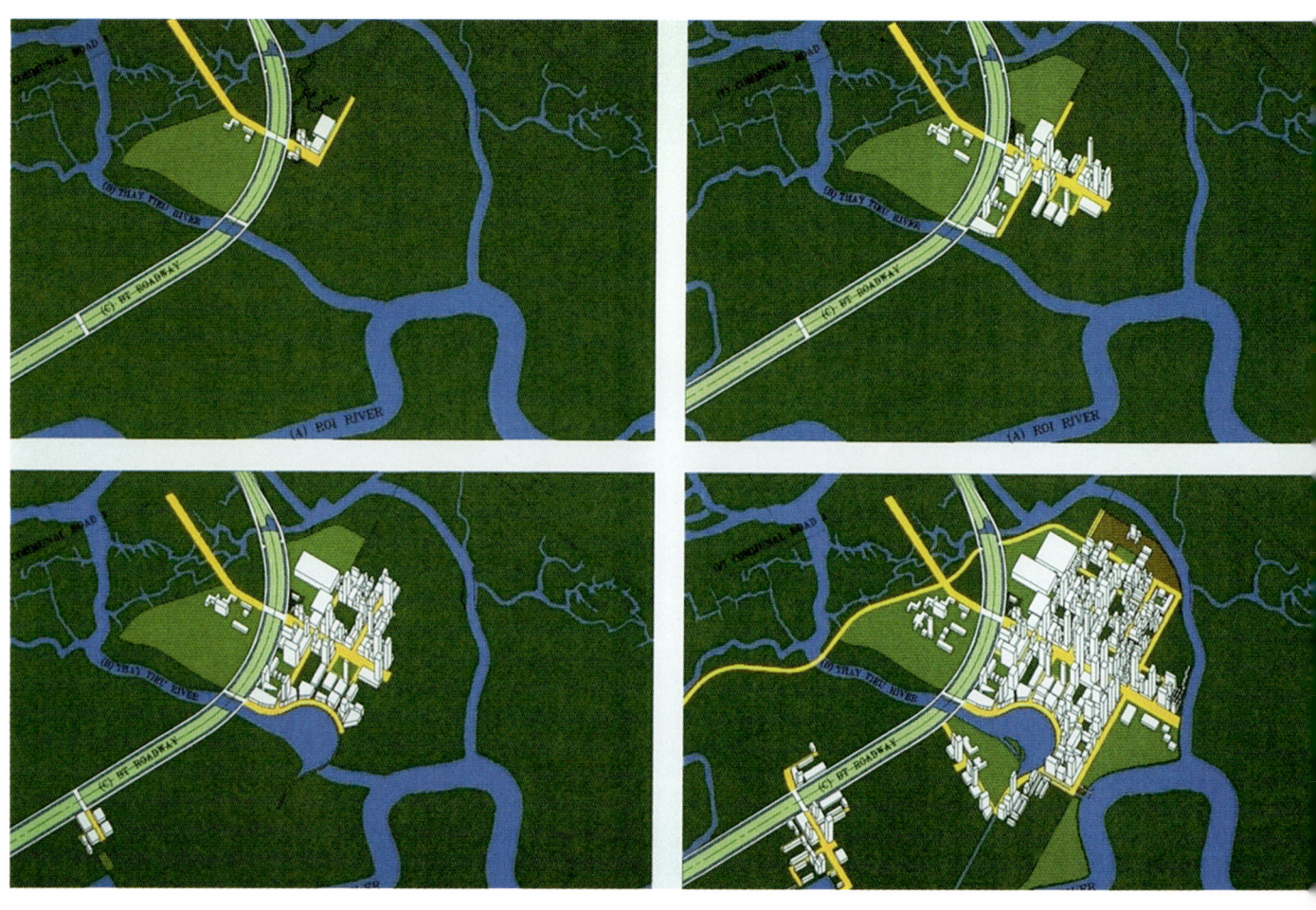

Asian cities, with most of the historic fabric eliminated. In Saigon South, the character of the old city, a place of rivers and canals, is the starting point for a new development in which walkable neighbourhoods are the base component. Water taxis as well as light rail systems will link the quarters in what is seen as 'a city of islands' – each island district will develop its own distinct character and sense of place. The islands are organised along the new east-west highway and a grid of north-west streets links the neighbourhoods. A strong emphasis is placed on open space and the retention of agricultural land around the new development quarters – sustainability was a plank of the project from the start.

The new city centre, phase I of Saigon South, is a mixed-use district, with five development areas over a 400-hectare (988-acre) site at the far east of Saigon South, close to the new port. The first buildings there were not architecturally distinguished, but the architecture is perhaps less important than the faithful implementation of a plan which avoids the pitfalls of other Asian centres.

left
The strategy for incremental growth of the new district - with a population of one million - includes the development of a new city centre. Beyond, new quarters will be served by new rail and waterbus systems.

right
Images reproduced in the Saigon South brochure emphasize easy transport links and pleasant public spaces.

LONDON
Canary Wharf

(1985-   )

Canary Wharf remains, many years after its inception, a highly contentious development, yet it is unquestionably the flagship of London's Docklands regeneration campaign. After a shaky start, the commercial success of the project is assured and construction work will extend well into the first decade of the 21st century. Its broader impact on London remains, however, a matter for debate. In particular, it remains to be seen whether Canary Wharf can transmute from an office ghetto into a mixed-use quarter and – even more in question – whether it can successfully integrate into the ongoing regeneration of East and South-east London.

The inspiration for Canary Wharf can be found in North America and more specifically in the World Financial Center in New York, developed by Olympia & York, the developer that brought the vision of G. Ware Travelstead to reality. The Manhattan scheme was nearly complete when O&Y took over Canary Wharf in 1987, inheriting a 1985 masterplan by Skidmore, Owings & Merrill. The site was part of the West India Docks, closed down in the 1970s as part of the general shutdown of London's docks. The Thatcher government had established the London Docklands Development Corporation in 1981 with the aim of encouraging new investment in the docklands – generous financial inducements and a generally laissez-faire approach to planning attracted developers. So too did the boom in the London office market following Stock Exchange deregulation ('the Big Bang') in 1986. Cautious planning policies in the City of London led developers to see huge potential outside the City's boundaries.

SOM's masterplan provided for a broadly Beaux-Arts format, with streets, squares and landscaped gardens, the latter designed rather formally in conjunction with Sir Roy Strong, with corporate taste in mind. The architecture of the first phases of the development was post-Modern Classical in manner, with SOM and Kohn Pedersen Fox designing the buildings, initially from the USA and with lots of heavy historicist detailing. Other architects involved in

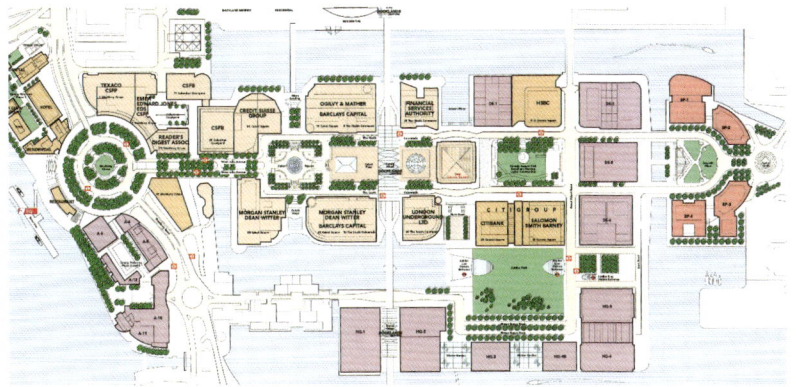

left
Canary Wharf, the
flagship of the
London Docklands
regeneration
programme, originated
in a 1985 masterplan
by SOM and is
likely to be completed
in the first decades of
the 21st century.

below
This plan by Richard
Rogers Partnership
for the development
of the Greenwich
peninsula shows
Canary Wharf (far
left) in the wider
context of the
regeneration of
southeast London.

the early stages included I. M. Pei, Troughton McAslan, Adamson Associates and Cesar Pelli. The landmark One Canada Square tower, completed in 1991, 244 metres (800 feet) high, with 112,000 square metres (1.2 million square feet) of offices and designed by Pelli, was, however, a distinctly modern monument. Pelli was also responsible for the impressive glazed station for the Docklands Light Railway, Canary Wharf's chief transport mode before the arrival, in 1999, of the Underground's Jubilee Line extension (JLE) – with an even more impressive station designed by Norman Foster.

The JLE came as a vital lifeline, since by 1999 Canary Wharf was the workplace for 25,000 people and the new link was urgently needed. The working population was predicted to rise to 42,000 by 2002 and to more than double again in a couple of decades. The

above
The site for Canary Wharf was part of the redundant West India Docks system, a few miles east of the City of London.

below and right
Initially, most of the buildings were designed by American architects, including Cesar Pelli, who was responsible for the central tower, One Canada Square, the tallest building in Europe at the time of its completion in 1991.

completion of the new Citibank London headquarters in 1999 (designed by Foster & Partners) and the announcement of two new towers, each over 90,000 square metres (1 million square feet) in area and rivalling One Canada Square, designed by Foster and Pelli, seemed to confirm that Canary Wharf's slow start – a consequence of the early Nineties recession – had been forgotten. The new architecture at Canary Wharf is firmly modern, though generally less than dramatic – the commercial style of the millennium. Foster's Citibank building, for example, looks bland alongside his superb Underground station.

Canary Wharf is, in fact, now a serious rival to the City in its own right and while the City has boxed itself into a planning package that seems to rule out large-scale re-development, Canary Wharf has land to spare. The Heron Quays development on the south of the estate will constitute a sizeable office city in its own right. Moreover, Canary Wharf is addressing accusations that it promotes an office mono-culture. Phase I of Canary Riverside – a 73,000-square-metre (786,000-square-foot) development of 322 luxury apartments, plus designer hotel, health club and restaurants – opened in 1999 and is ongoing. Anti-Canary Wharf lobbyists have complained that 'this is a very private estate', pointing out that nothing of the genuinely public space created in New York's Battery Park City has emerged here. Critics maintain that this is a world apart, policed and cut off from the life of the East End. While the project has been hugely subsidized by the public purse – not least in the provision of the vital Underground link – the Canary Wharf Group argues that it is working hard to inject some of this wealth back into the local community. The Group supports study centres in several nearby schools, as well as a number of sports teams. In its committment to provide jobs the Canary Wharf Group has set up employment initiatives in conjunction with the local authority and placed over £100 million of contracts with local businesses. Londoners will watch with interest to see the longterm results.

The architectural character of the project was at first predominantly post-Modernist (left), but Foster & Partners' HSBC tower (right) is straightforwardly modernist in character.

The third of the clump of towers at the heart of Canary Wharf has been designed, like One Canada Square, by Cesar Pelli (left). The adjacent Citibank building (right, completed 1999) was designed by Foster & Partners and overlooks a new urban park.

Jubilee line

Foster & Partners'
new Underground
station is on the
scale of a mainline
terminal and designed
to handle a working
population set to
double within a
decade. The
Underground
connection opened
only in 1999 – Canary
Wharf had previously
suffered from limited
transport
connections.

↑ Jubilee line

ALMERE
Masterplan

(1995-2005)

The new town of Almere, near Amsterdam, has existed for only two decades, but already has a population of 100,000. Its architectural record is one of innovation and imagination, so that the commission (the result of a competition in 1994–5) to Rem Koolhaas of OMA to masterplan the new city centre of Almere came as no surprise. Almere needs a real centre, since it is emerging from a group of linked neighbourhoods, each with its own shops and public buildings, to become a true city. As such, it needs a commercial heart and the cultural amenities that help to define civic existence.

Almere already has a developed road and rail system – the existing central station is an obvious node of growth, since there are undeveloped sites close at hand. North of the station, Koolhaas proposes a large (130,000-square-metre/1.4 million-square-foot) office complex which will be the focus for new employment in the city. The office complex is deliberately dense, with a high-rise component, so as to free up land for the public buildings – theatre, concert hall, library and art school south of the tracks. A broad boulevard here forms a cultural axis.

The mix of uses in the masterplan includes 1,100 residential units and 53,000 square metres (570,000 square feet) of commercial development – a massive enhancement of the existing provision.

right
Koolhaas's 1994 masterplan for the new city centre of Almere imposes an urban format on a settlement of distinct neighbourhoods, which has previously lacked a heart.

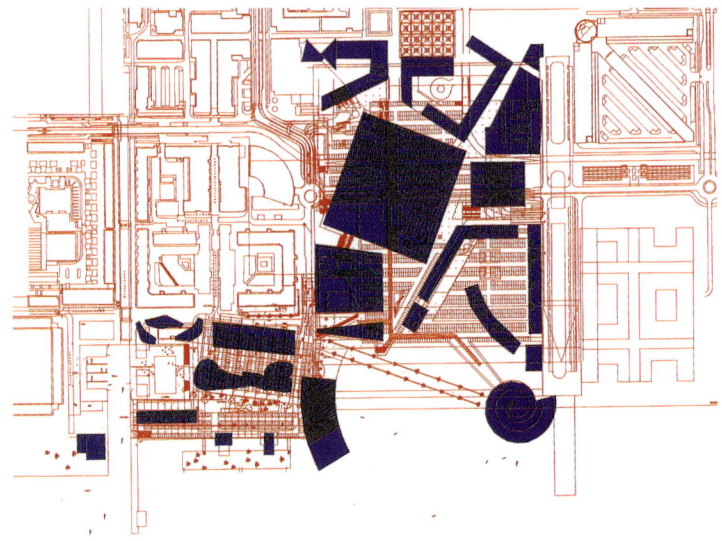

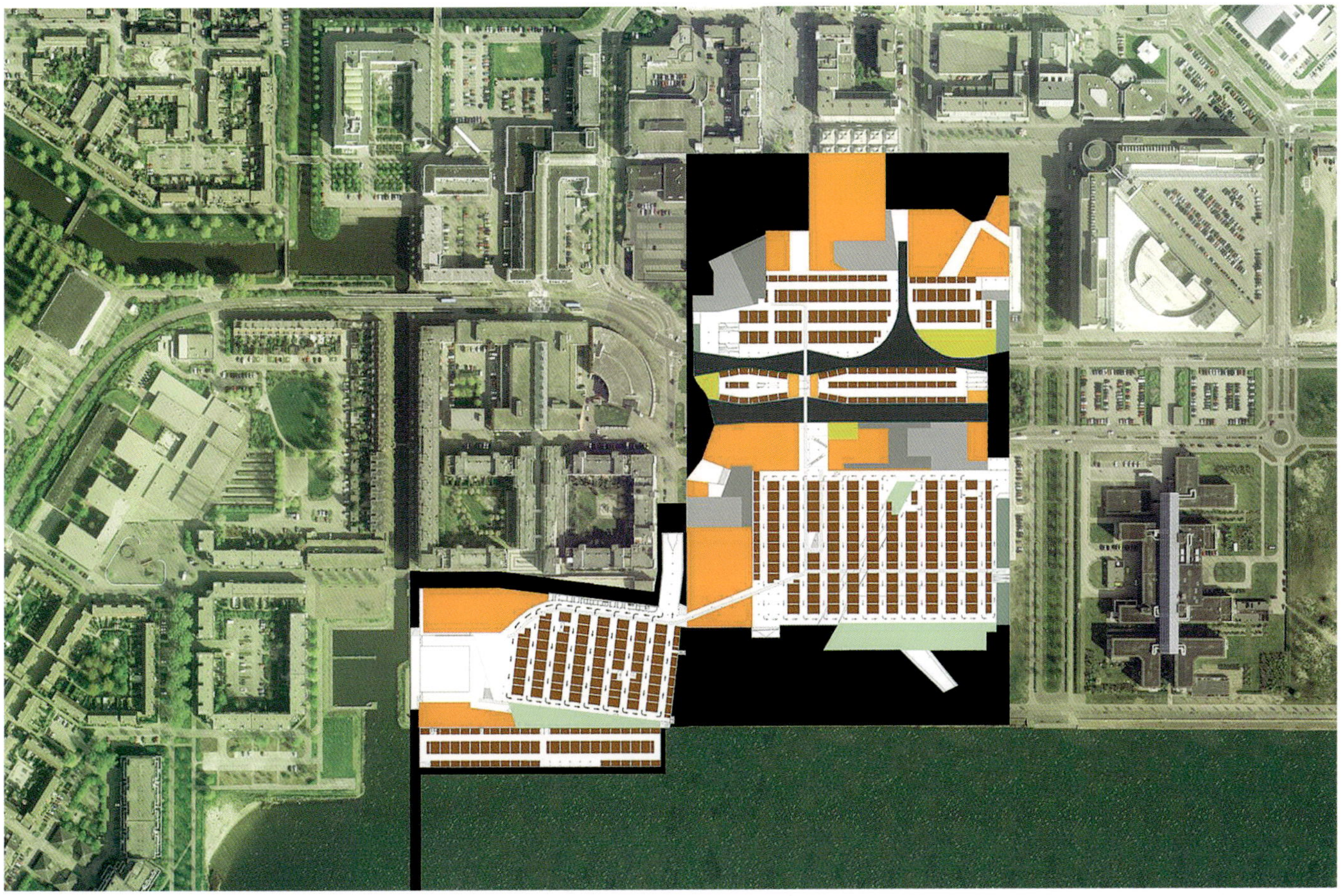

The masterplan is
about intensifying
the urban form of
Almere and adding new
layers of activity in
what is virtually a
megastructure. The
city wants to acquire
a skyline, breaking
its lowrise profile.

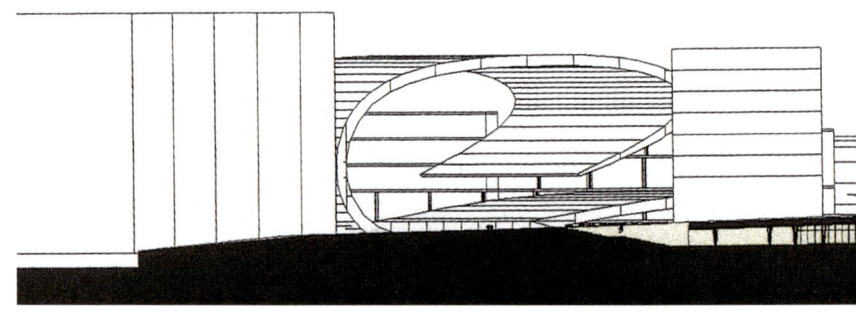

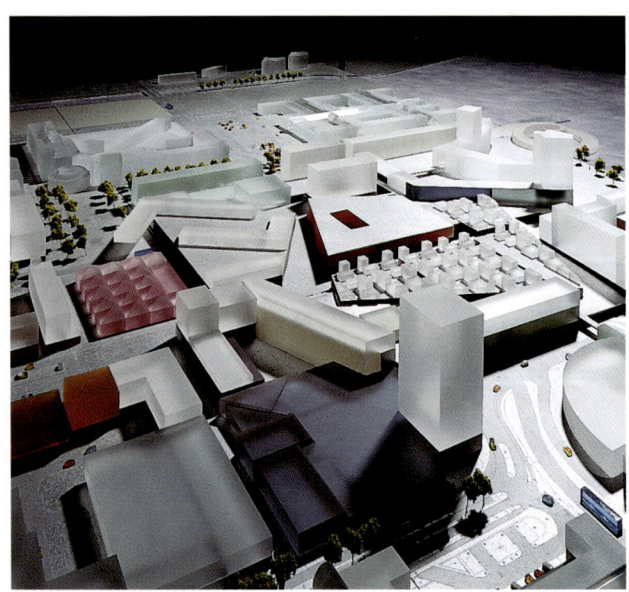

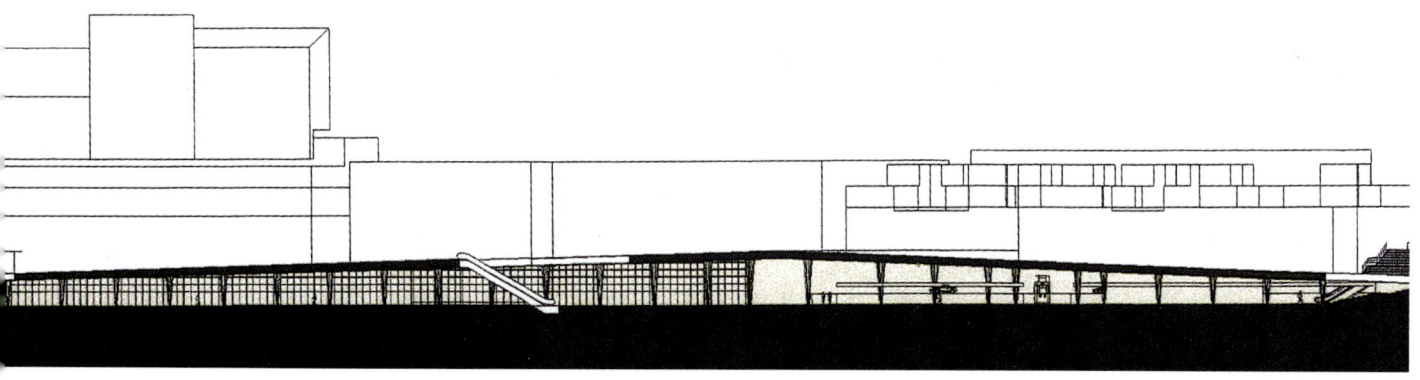

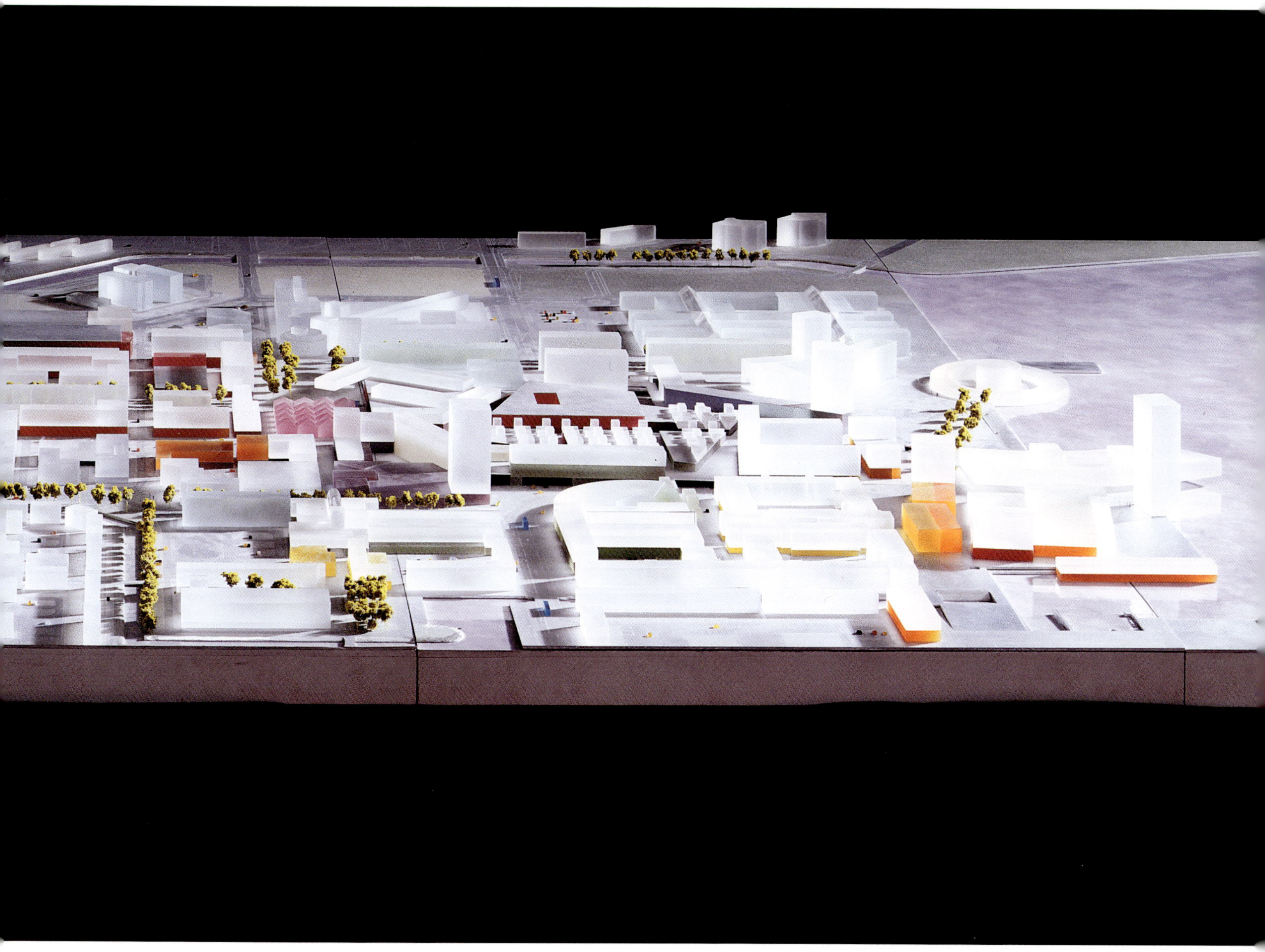

The existing
character of Almere
is one of relatively
high density but low
intensity, though
the area around the
Central Station
(right) is the
obvious focus of
the new city.

ROTTERDAM
Kop van Zuid

(1987-2010)

Rotterdam's Kop van Zuid project is one of the most ambitious schemes of urban extension in Europe, notable not only for its emphasis on mixed use and the necessity of fully integrating the new quarter with the existing city centre – issues sometimes sidestepped or ignored in developments of this nature – but equally for the high quality of the new architecture it has generated.

Badly damaged in the Second World War and subsequently the subject of one of Europe's most heroic reconstruction programmes, Rotterdam remains one of the great ports of the world. However, as in London, Genoa and New York, the changing needs of the shipping industry have left large areas of former dockland redundant. The site for Kop van Zuid consists of 125 hectares (309 acres) of reclaimed land around Binnenhaven, Entrepothaven and Wilhelminapier, once the heart of the port, now bypassed in favour of more accessible sites (the Europort and Maasvlakte) far removed from central Rotterdam. The south bank of the river Maas, seen as the obvious place for the city to grow, actually remained virtually undeveloped until the 1860s, when the leading merchant Lodewijk Pincoffs promoted the development of the area – which became the centre of Rotterdam's maritime trade, a booming quarter of dockers, seamen, merchants and travellers. The Wilhelminapier, for example, was the point of departure for the Holland America Line's (HAL) North American service, with a magnificent headquarters building for the Line at its tip. The post-war era saw the area decline into increasing dereliction – prostitution became so endemic that there was even a proposal to establish a licensed red-light quarter there. (The idea was quashed after public protests.) The only serious option seemed to be the construction of large tracts of social housing, linked to existing housing areas south of the docks.

A change in direction came in the mid-1980s, when the area began to be seen as a potential extension of the city centre,

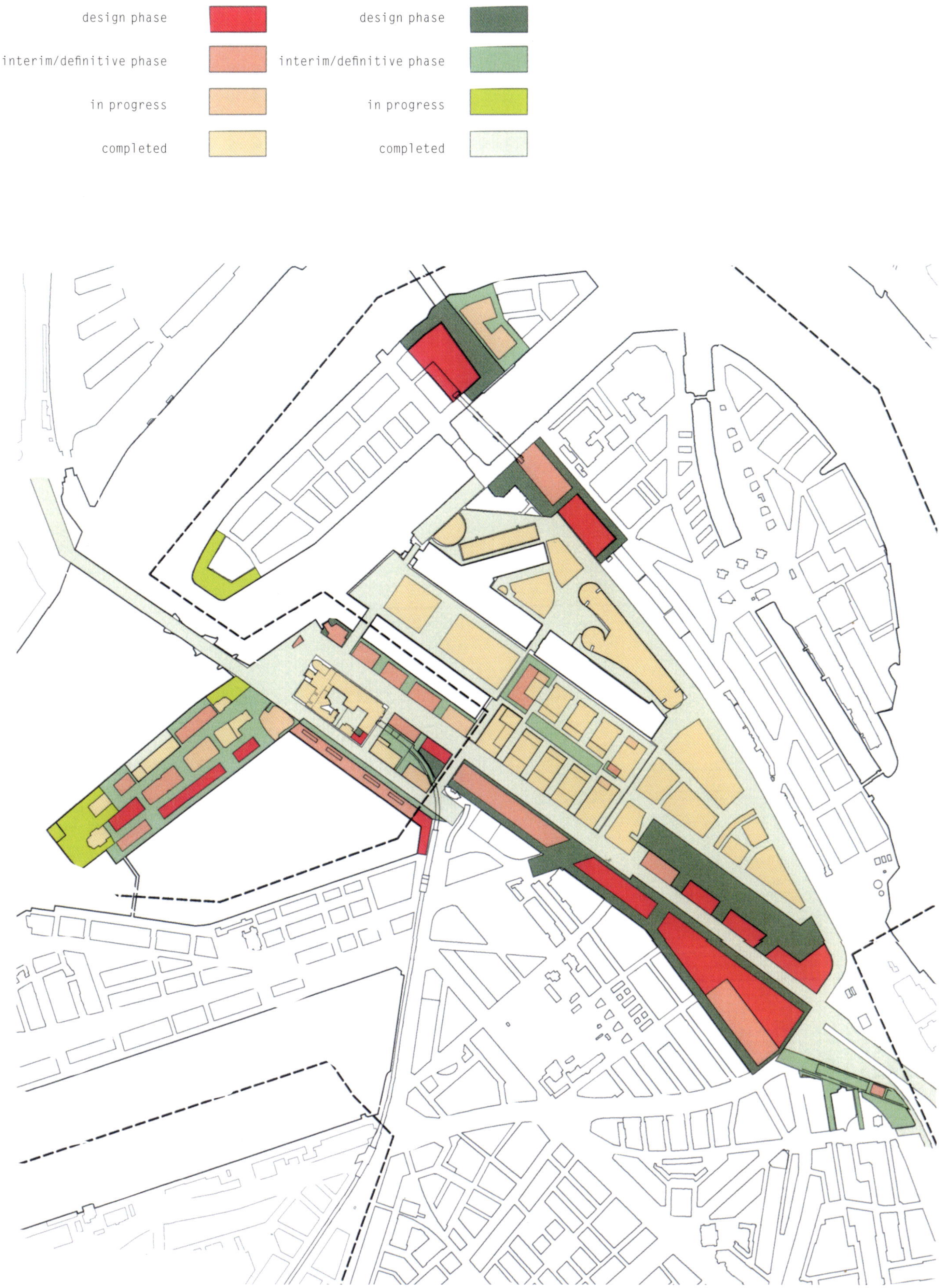
design phase
interim/definitive phase
in progress
completed
design phase
interim/definitive phase
in progress
completed

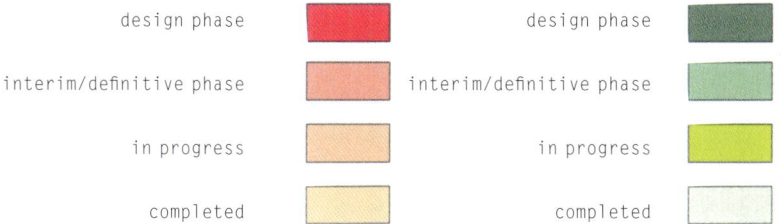

Bolles-Wilson's
Bridgewatcher's
House (right) and
the associated
landscaping around
the Erasmus Bridge
(left) typifies the
innovative approach
to design at Kop
van Zuid.

addressing Rotterdam's requirements for high quality commercial and residential developments. Kop van Zuid had already been the subject of masterplanning proposals (1982) by Aldo Rossi, O.M. Ungers and others, which envisaged a dense and highly regular layout of new avenues, streets and urban blocks. Teun Koolhaas's masterplan of 1987, commissioned by the city authorities with the charismatic Riek Bakker as Director of Urban Development, provided a more flexible approach to future development. Somewhat amended in 1991, it has served as the basis for the reconstruction of Kop van Zuid. A land use plan was the foundation of the project, with around 5,300 new residential units, 370,000 square metres

Van Berkel & Bos's
Erasmus Bridge,
opened in 1996, was
a vital part of
the transport
infrastructure which
linked Kop van Zuid to
central Rotterdam,
but has also served
as a symbol of
regeneration.

(4 million square feet) of offices and 90,000 square metres (1 million square feet) of light industrial, educational and leisure space. The free market approach taken at London's Canary Wharf – a planner-free 'enterprise zone', where the developers produced their own masterplan – was ruled out in favour of a prescriptive planning framework, with scope for developers to work freely within its guidelines. It was a plan 'that uses, to the utmost, the spatial possibilities of the area and its immediate vicinity, that programmatically links up perfectly to the developments in Rotterdam's economy and housing market and that combines, in its manifestation, the business-like character and bravura of Rotterdam'.

A basic requirement of the Koolhaas plan was enhanced communications to link Kop van Zuid more firmly to the city centre across the Maas. Van Berkel & Bos's stunning Erasmus Bridge opened in 1996, providing not only a physical connection but also serving as a dramatic symbol of regeneration – it could be seen as the key move in the entire project. The bridge is connected to a new boulevard traversing the area. A new metro station opened the following year.

The scope of the masterplan to embrace a variety of architectural approaches is reflected in Norman Foster's plans for the Wilhelminapier (1992), where half the office accommodation, and a substantial proportion of the housing, in Kop van Zuid is to be located. Designed to be phased over 15 years (1995–2010) Foster's plan incorporates retained historic structures, including the splendid HAL building (now converted into the New York Hotel) and major new buildings, including a clump of high-rise towers. The Wilhelminapier forms a transitional zone between the city centre and the further reaches of the former docklands, so that dense commercial and residential development is appropriate. One of the first new buildings, the Marine Safety Centre (completed 1994), was designed by Foster & Partners, though other sites were to be subject to design competitions.

left
The Marine Safety Centre was the first new building to be completed under Foster & Partners' masterplan for the Wilheminapier – the Foster plan is phased over 15 years.

right
The Luxor Cinema by Bolles - Wilson is part of a series of new cultural facilities in the area.

Foster & Partners were selected for the 37,000-square-metre (400,000-square-foot), 32-storey, twin-tower World Port Centre scheduled for completion in 2000. Another high-rise block is being designed by Renzo Piano.

Architects Bolles-Wilson have been responsible for a series of projects, including the striking Bridgewatchers' House, a control building for the Erasmus Bridge, and landscaping around the bridge at Wilhemina Quay. Bolles-Wilson won first prize in the competition for the New Luxor Cinema in 1996. Wrapped in a tomato-red cladding, the theatre is scheduled for completion in 2000 and will be a dynamic expression of the ambition to make Kop van Zuid a lively cultural quarter, part of an arts circuit that extends to the Schouwburgplein (see pages 236–41)

The public-private partnership basis on which Kop van Zuid is being developed has ensured that broad social and economic issues can be addressed, alongside the agenda of the market. The 600 houses and apartments in the Landtong quarter include many units for rent. In Stadstuinen the housing is deliberately mixed income and aimed at families. Here and in the Vuurplat, shops and schools are close at hand. Albeda College in the Parkzicht quarter, at the southern end of the Kop van Zuid, is one of the largest vocational training centres in the country. Closer to the city centre, the Entrepot area includes much specialist shopping, including a festival market, as well as luxury housing. The state has underwritten the project not only by investing hugely in infrastructure but also by locating public agencies in Kop van Zuid – the 75,000 square-metre (800,000-square-foot) Wilhelminahof office complex for tax and customs authorities is the most prominent example (though Cees Dam's buildings are architecturally disappointing).

Kop van Zuid was emerging from the dust of construction at the end of the 20th century as a real extension of the city, not a place apart. It seemed that the dreams of the 19th-century builders of the port, which evaporated in the post-war years, might finally come to fruition.

left and below
The 'Hillekop 3' housing project by Mecanoo architects.

right, top and bottom
Albeda College by Bolles-Wilson.

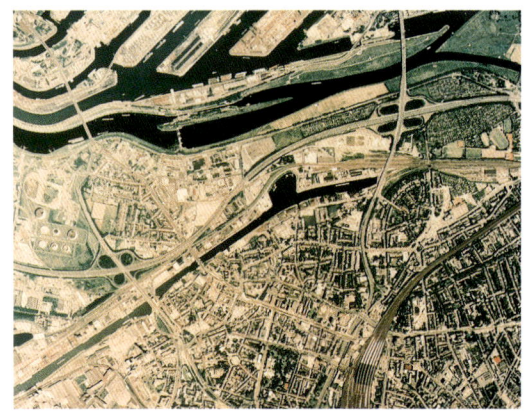

DUISBURG
Inner Harbour

(1991-   )

Duisburg is located, at the junction of the rivers Rhine and Ruhr, in the epicentre of Germany's 19th-century heavy industrial region. In recent years, the region's once dominant steel industry has contracted – the coal mining industry has also declined hugely. By the late Eighties, unemployment levels were amongst the worst in Germany. The 1991 competition, won by Foster & Partners, for the masterplanning of the once busy – but now largely redundant – Inner Harbour as a centre of economic regeneration reflected the city and region's determination to counter the effects of industrial change.

By selecting the Inner Harbour as a focus for urban renewal, Duisburg capitalized on one of its greatest assets – the 1.8-kilometre (just over one mile) long basin is, in fact, the largest inland harbour in the world, but had always been cut off from the city centre. The 89-hectare (220-acre) development site included a number of old warehouses with potential for reuse, alongside swathes of empty land – the ideal mix.

The subject of a public/private partnership, the Inner Harbour project was designed for phased development over several decades. Environmental and infrastructure issues were crucial to its success. The once heavily polluted harbour system is being systematically cleaned to make it a habitat for fish and to encourage its use for leisure. A dam, carrying a new road, was constructed across the harbour in 1998–9, so that the level of the water can be maintained – beyond the dam, levels fluctuate by up to 7 metres (23 feet) with the tidal flow of the Rhine. The potential of the harbour for recreational use has thus been transformed. South of the new 'lake', three new canals were cut (in 1997–9) to form an attractive setting for housing developments – they are filled by means of pumped groundwater, supplemented by filtered rainwater. The first housing blocks have already been completed – the aim is to secure a social balance, with blocks of low-cost housing for rent.

Along the north side of the Inner Harbour, the Euro Gate development is designed to house

The Inner Harbour at Duisburg is the largest inland harbour in the world and became a key asset in the regeneration of an industrial city hit by the decline of its steel and coal industries.

offices, a hotel, shops, restaurants, and apartments. The strong environmental agenda behind the masterplan is reflected in Euro Gate's massive array of photovoltaic generators – the largest installation anywhere.

The masterplan actively encourages public access to the whole regenerated quarter (a contrast, for example, to the essentially private and fragmented character of many of London's Docklands developments). Along the western edge of the Inner Harbour, a 660 metre- (2,165 foot-) long pedestrian promenade has been laid out. Nearby, the Steiger Schwanentour (completed 1994) provides mooring facilities for Rhine tourist boats through a series of floating pontoons.

Creative conversion of existing buildings is another major element in the project. The first reuse project to be completed was the Hafenforum, formerly a grain warehouse but converted by Foster & Partners into the headquarters of the development corporation that is running the entire Inner Harbour project, along with lettable offices and a restaurant. The conversion was seen as the exemplar for other such schemes and combines careful retention of existing features with more radical interventions – the use of glazed partitions, for example, to create flexible space. Other warehouses are likely to be used for housing, offices and as workshops for artists and craftsmen.

The Inner Harbour project builds on the proven success of other waterfront developments in Europe and North America, while introducing innovative elements that make it a point of reference for other such projects in the 21st century.

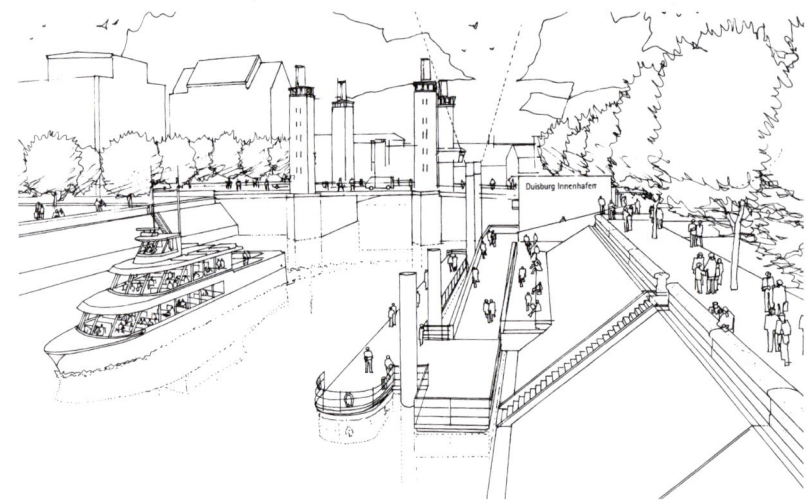

left
By damming the
harbour, a constant
water level has been
achieved, encouraging
leisure uses.

right and below
A series of canals
permeates the
development site
around the harbour,
providing attractive
sites for housing.

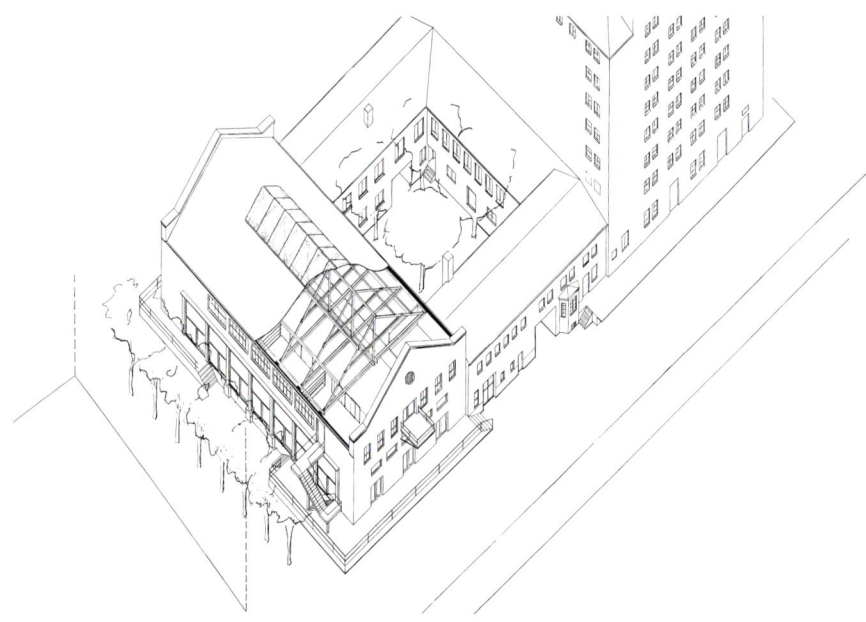

The Hafenforum, a converted warehouse, contains the offices of the development corporation and is seen as the model for the reuse of other surviving industrial buildings.

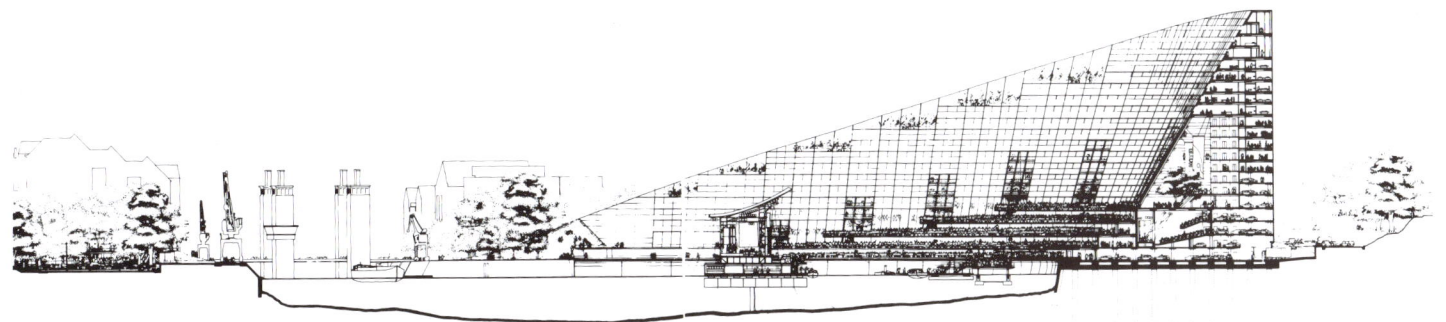

right
Foster & Partners'
multi-use Euro Gate
is intended as the
landmark building in
the Inner Harbour
project and is as
environmentally
friendly as it is
architecturally
striking.

left
A design for a duplex
apartment building by
Foster & Partners.
The goal has been to
provide housing for a
range of incomes.

NEW YORK
Battery Park City

(1979-2000)

The Battery Park City project has regenerated a large waterfront site, close to the Financial District of Manhattan, and opened it up for public use.

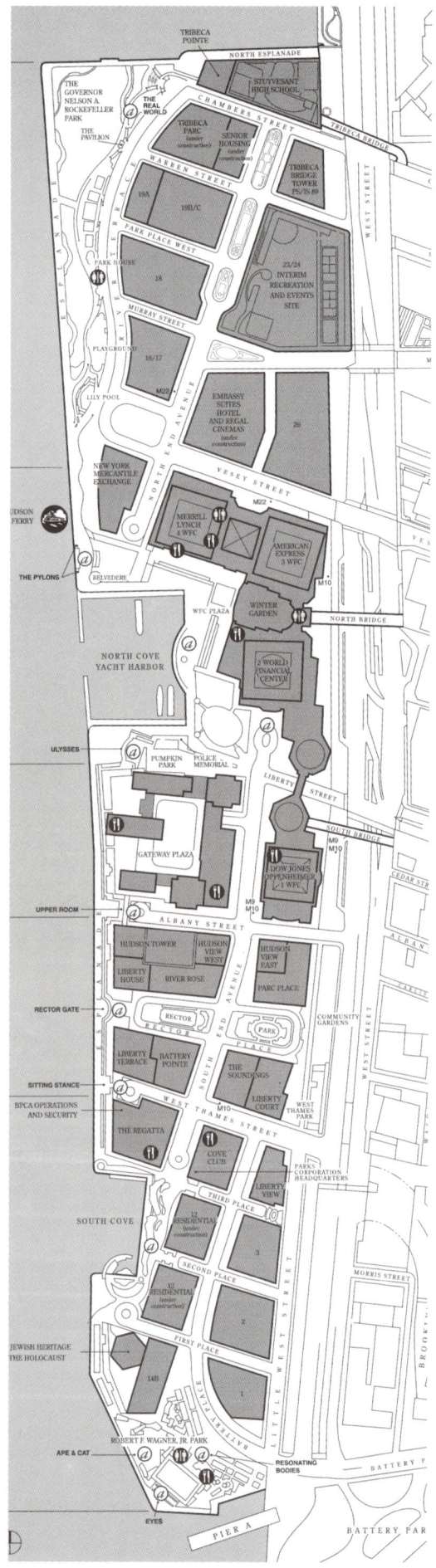

Battery Park City had its origins in the 1960s, when the decay of Manhattan's historic port was already well advanced. The outcome was large areas of vacant land and docks, formerly filled with wharves, railway yards and transit sheds, which formed an impenetrable barrier between the city and the waterfront. The 37-hectare (92-acre) site alongside the Hudson river at Battery Park was first designated as a development area in 1966, a significant augmentation of the crowded island of Manhattan which would bring new jobs and investment to the Lower West Side. The first task was to landfill the former docks – this had been completed by 1976, but the city's late Seventies financial crisis brought the entire project to a halt. In 1979, it was revived in earnest, with a restructured Battery Park City Authority, appointed by the State of New York, and a new masterplan by Alexander Cooper and Stanton Eckstut. Previous ideas of a vast megastructure, elevated above ground level, were jettisoned in favour of an extension of the existing street grid at grade. The site would thus be parcelled into typical New York blocks, which could be developed individually or in groups.

From the beginning, the giant scheme combined office and residential development (including 'social' housing) and was intended to produce an integrated city quarter – 550,000 square metres (6 million square feet) of offices was planned and housing for up to 14,000 people. Significant areas of public space, including parks and recreation areas serving the entire city, were an important feature. Work began on Gateway Plaza, a 1,700-unit residential scheme at the centre of the elongated site, in 1980. In the following year, developer Olympia & York began constructing the World Financial Center to plans by Cesar Pelli – six office towers, each of around 90,000 square metres (one million square feet), with a spectacular glazed Winter Garden containing shopping and restaurants and looking over a riverside square. (The WFC, completed in 1988, was, of course, the prototype for London's even larger Canary Wharf development and stands

left
The 1979 masterplan
was based on the idea
of extending the grid
of the city – earlier
plans for an elevated
megastructure were
abandoned.

right and below
The project provides
for substantial areas
of public open space
– a rare commodity
in Manhattan.

Pelli's World
Financial Center,
built from 1981 to
1988, gave Battery
Park City a 558,000
square metre (six
million square foot)
office base.

somewhat apart from the remainder of the project.) Development continued throughout the 1990s and Battery Park City was scheduled to have assumed its final form by the first year of the new century.

The essence of Battery Park City is its foundation in well-tried urban forms. While the office buildings take the form of dumpy skyscrapers (overshadowed by the nearby World Trade Center), the residential blocks are typically of seven to ten storeys, set directly on to the street and recalling countless other blocks in, for example, 5th Avenue, Gramercy Park and the Upper East Side. The blocks are generally faced in brick, with stone bases, and with retailing at street level. Very close attention has been given to the design of paving, street surfaces, lighting and planting. A large group of architectural practices has been charged with the realization of the strict design guidelines, producing architecture which is essentially pragmatic and undemonstrative.

Nonetheless, the formula proved attractive and by 1995 9,500 residents had moved in, joining over 30,000 office workers. Criticisms that the area is a professional ghetto, a highly priced adjunct to Wall Street, do not take account of its wider benefits – the riverside public esplanade, 12 hectares (30 acres) of public parks, Roche Dinkeloo's Holocaust Museum (opened 1997) and active public art programme. The first public school in the area (Stuyvestant High School, with 3,000 pupils) opened in 1998 – a 'magnet' school designed for academic high-flyers particularly in the sciences. The residential sites have now been almost entirely taken up – one of the last was filled by one of a few residential towers, the 42-storey Tribeca Pointe, next to Stuyvestant High School (both were designed by Gruzen Samton), which forms a dramatic northern termination to Battery Park City. There is, however, no 'social' housing, though profits from the development have been channelled into housing projects elsewhere in the city.

Despite its continuing isolation from the city by an eight-lane freeway, Battery Park City

has become a well-liked amenity for New
Yorkers and a lung for workers in the Financial
District . If the architecture seems too polite and
too uniform, it reflects an increasing desire in
New York for a revival of civic design and the
imposition of firm guidelines on development.
It is the public space here that is, without
question, the great success.

Residential blocks address streets and public riverfront promenades. Great care has been taken with planting and street furniture.

left, top and bottom
The office element
of the project is
surrounded by public
space, with access to
the waterfront.

right
The New York
Mercantile Exchange,
by Skidmore, Owings
and Merrill.

KUALA LUMPUR
International
airport, city
centre and
Eco-media city

(1992-   )

The new Kuala Lumpur international airport (opened in 1998) is a major, city-sized project in its own right, intended as one of the three major Asian hubs for air travel in the 21st century. Kisho Kurokawa was appointed architect for the terminal building in 1992 and work began on site in 1995. Initially, the airport caters for 25 million passengers annually, rising to 60 million by 2020, though further phases of development will equip it to handle 125 million, plus large quantities of freight. The site is larger (at 10,000 hectares/25,000 acres) than that of any of the competing Asian airports, including Chek Lap Kok. Designed to cope with an impending age of mass supersonic travel, the new airport is equally calculated to strengthen the position of Kuala Lumpur as one of the world's leading business centres. By 2020, Malaysia expects to assume the role of a fully 'developed' nation.

The architectural form of the airport buildings is, as one would expect, somewhat removed from the lightweight, high-tech mould of Foster's Chek Lap Kok or Piano's Kansai. The terminal building is topped by a dramatically formed concrete shell roof which is explicitly intended to evoke the characteristic oil palm plantations that are a prominent feature of the surrounding landscape. The great granite-clad columns that frame the entrance to the building are equally evocative of nature and of Asian and Islamic tradition and their monumental form is extended into the interior of the terminal. In the kilometre-long pier that connects the terminal to the satellite, the architectural language is lighter and this mood continues into the satellite, cruciform in plan with a heavily planted central garden. Kuala Lumpur has acquired one of the most idiosyncratic and most memorable of modern air terminals.

The new airport is 60 kilometres (37 miles) south of the centre of Kuala Lumpur – a deliberate move, since a new city, the Kuala Lumpur linear capital corridor, a centre for new multi-media industries, is to be developed between the two. It is planned to move

Kuala Lumpur's development strategy for the 21st century provides for a new 'capital corridor' linking the old city centre to the new international airport. The satellite city of Putrajaya has been designated as the new federal capital.

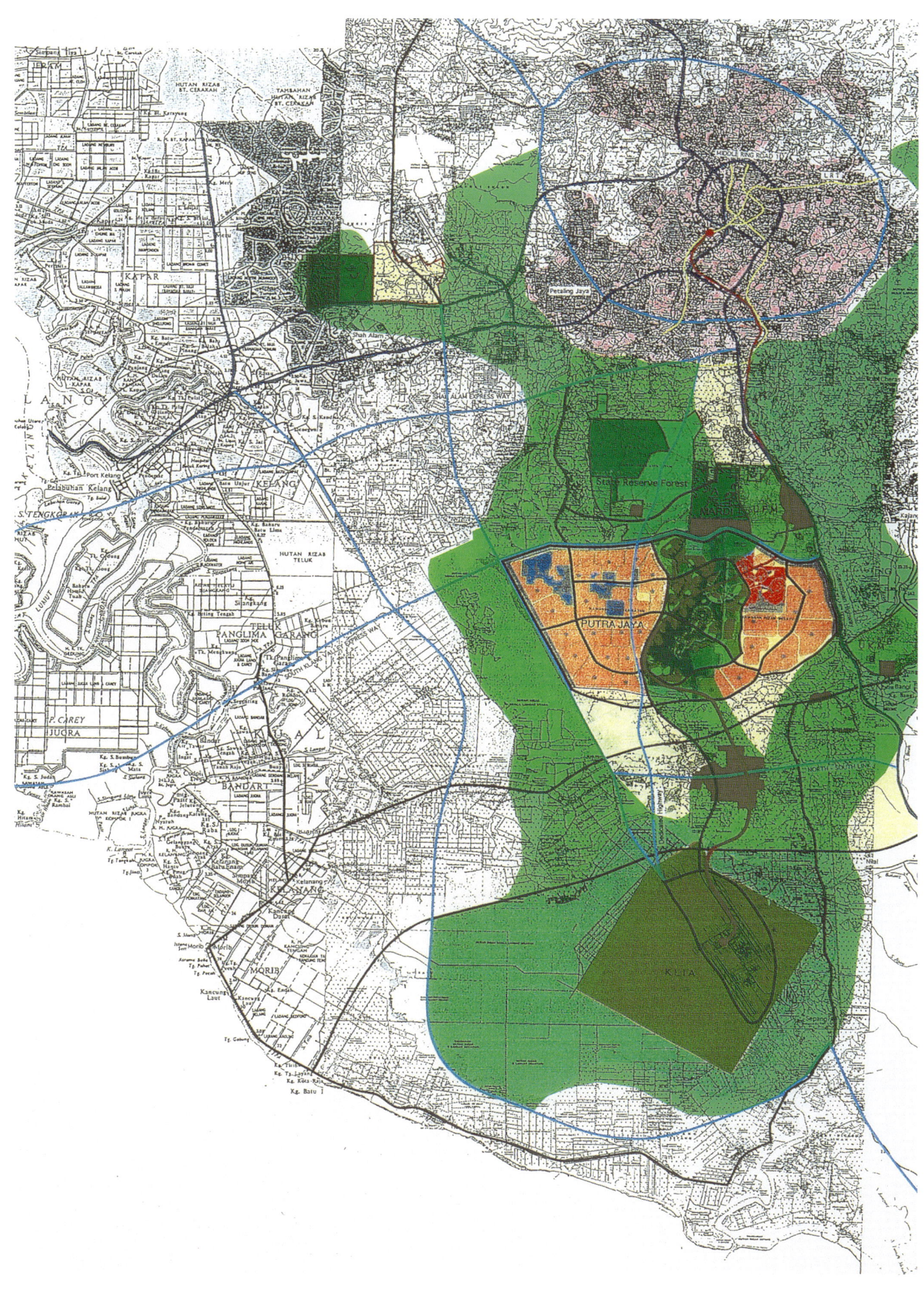

government functions to the intermediate
settlement of Putrajaya, designated as the new
federal capital, with a workforce of 150,000
people. Information traffic is the backbone of
the new, 14-kilometre- (9-mile-) wide, 'multi-
media super-corridor' zone, which also carries
new high-speed road and rail links.

Kuala Lumpur is not an ancient city: it came
into existence only in the 1850s and much of its
built fabric is late 19th-century in date. The old
city centre is itself undergoing major changes.
The Kuala Lumpur City Centre development,
masterplanned by Klages, Carter, Vail & Partners
on the site of a former racecourse includes over
1.7 million square metres (18 million square
feet) of space in 20 buildings, the most
prominent of them Cesar Pelli's 452-metre
(1,485-foot) tall Petronas Towers, which
themselves (allegedly) pay homage to the
traditional architectural forms of the region.
Though striking in form, the Towers (built
1993–8) could be seen as a reflection of the
rush to embrace high-energy Western
technologies at the expense of the environment.

Kurokawa's concept of an eco-media city
merges (in a symbiosis, as Kurokawa likes to
call it) the needs of the natural environment
and of a changing human society. New
settlements will be interspersed with large areas
of new forest. Kurokawa's interest in

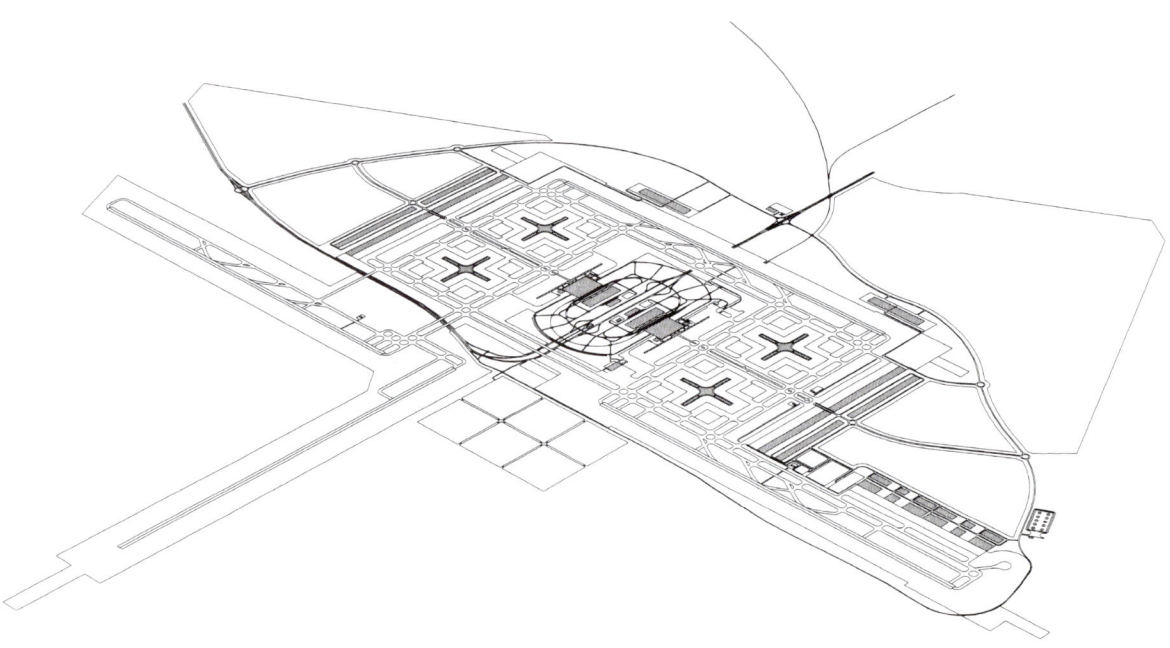

Kisho Kurokawa's
international
airport, begun in
1995, is designed to
expand to cater for
125 million
passengers annually.
Its strikingly
expressive canopies
echo nearby oil-palm
plantations .

reconciling nature and technology extends back 30 years, to the time when he was a leader of the Metabolist movement and developed the idea of the Eco-city. The Eco-media cities of the 21st century will be 'a network of small, high-density cities situated in the midst of natural habitats such as forests, pastures, and seashores... They will be supported by advanced technology, yet at the same time be cities capable of symbiosis with animals and birds in the forest'. Kurokawa argues that the genetic resources of the Malaysian rain forest will be the basis for new and hugely profitable bio-technological enterprises – therefore the protection of the natural environment will be the key to future prosperity. It remains to be seen how far these prescriptions guide the developing linear city. For the moment, the man-made forests around the new airport are the most striking expression of symbiosis and of the concern in the new urbanism for nature.

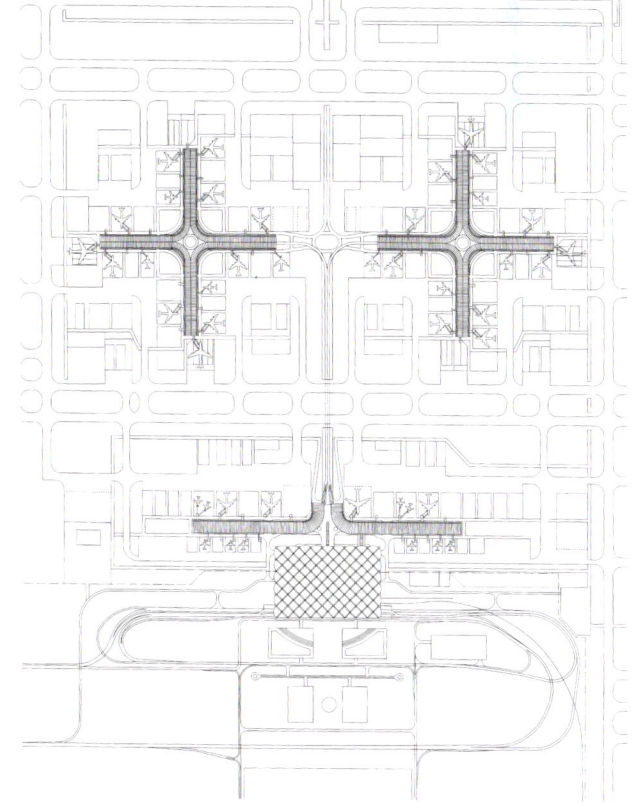

Kurokawa's terminal
draws on a number of
sources, including
western High-tech,
but is unique in its
incorporation of
gardens while dense
plantations around
the airport tie it
to the established
landscape.

SANTA CRUZ, TENERIFE
Link Quay

(1998–   )

Tenerife, in the Canary Islands, feels like an outpost of Europe, stranded in the Atlantic. This is its attraction as an escapist holiday location, yet the island is anxious to improve its links with the outside world and broaden its economy. These aims underlay the 1998 competition for developing the marina and harbour of Santa Cruz, won by Herzog & de Meuron.

The dramatic form of Tenerife reflects the island's volcanic origins and many centuries in which its shores have been eroded by the Atlantic waves. Instead of swathes of easily accessible beaches, there is often an abrupt transition from land to sea, with steep cliffs between. 'The relation between sea and land', write Herzog & de Meuron, 'is not built in horizontal layers but in singular gestures, comparable to sudden, natural events'. Herzog & de Meuron see their Santa Cruz project as a 'singular, urbanistic gesture... a gesture of embracing and enclosing'. The Link Quay is not a built object stranded in front of the existing sea front of the city, but a continuation of the city to provide a new public space. The 600-boat marina will form part of a sequence of urban spaces, from the Plaza Candelaria to the ocean. Approached from the sea, the marina will appear as 'a magic piece of garden sitting in front of the city and the steep mountains. It will attract you like an oasis in the sea'.

The new quay will be constructed on existing breakwaters, from which the new walkways and low-rise buildings (carrying rooftop walkways) will rise and will be

top right
This refreshingly simple initial sketch summarizes the intentions of the project's designers.

right
Tenerife has a dramatic, volcanic landscape (bottom). The city of Santa Cruz badly needs a more usable waterfront and Herzog and de Meuron's New Link Quay project addresses this issue.

Cutting out a piece from the Atlantic

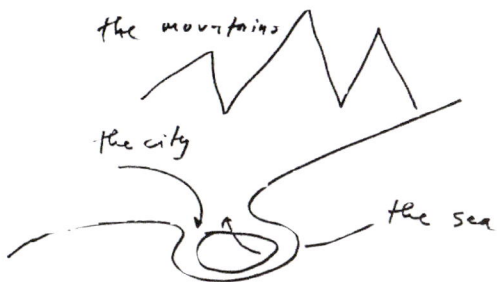

the mountains

the city   the sea

Plaza Candelaria

Plaza de España

Arena

connected by ramps to the Avenida Maritima. The ramps will be broad enough to carry parking, as well as forming welcoming boulevards into the development. Beyond, the Arena, built on the site of the ancient fortress of Santa Cruz, will be a generous new public square, a place for socializing and a venue for events of every sort. Close to the marina, the Los Llanos industrial area is seen as a location for future city growth, with a first phase concentrating on the development of the seafront between the marina and the Barranco de Santos creek.

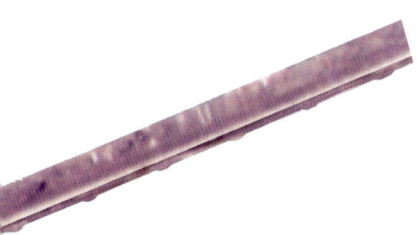

The new quay is a continuation of the existing city grain and provides for a new marina plus generous public spaces overlooking the ocean.

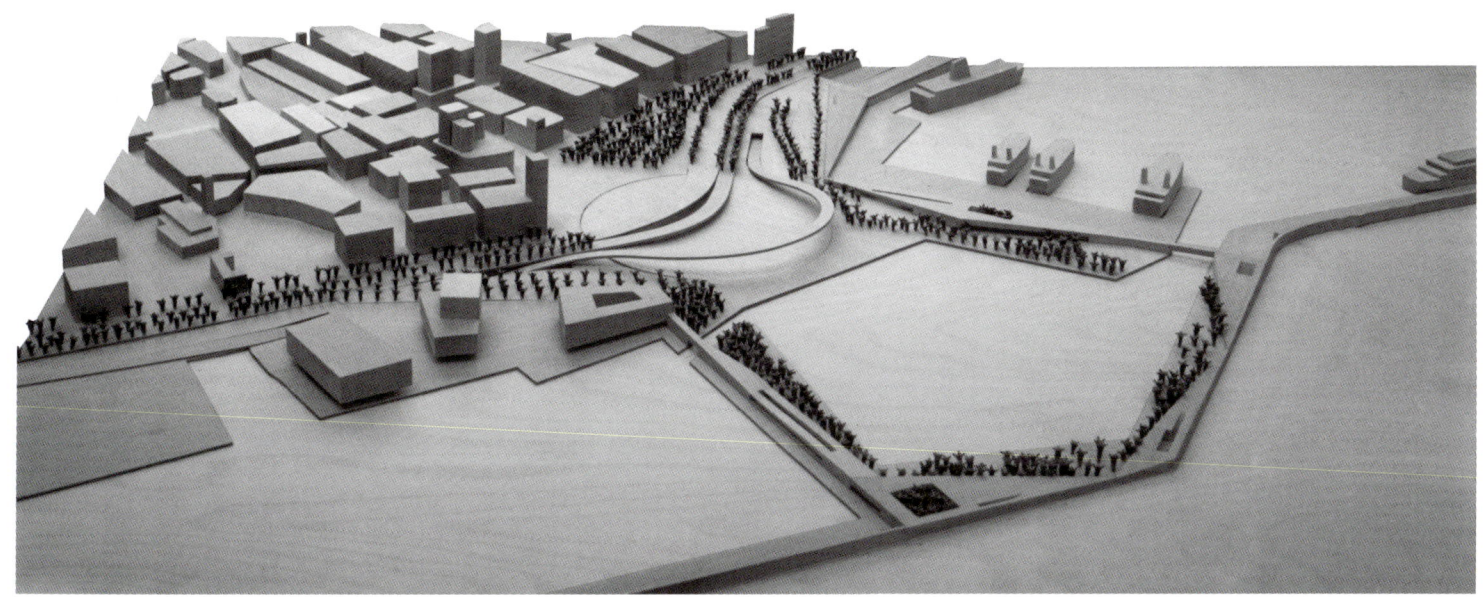

Cities
in
Motion

The modern city had its origins in the railway age. Rail
transport revolutionized local travel, creating a new class
of commuters, confirming the dominance of capitals such as Paris,
London and Berlin - which became the hubs of national rail
systems - over their provincial satellites and making the
fortunes of other big centres (such as Chicago, the great mart
of the mid-West, the true heartland of the USA). The great city
stations - the Gare du Nord, St Pancras, Grand Central, Roma
Termini - were hailed as the modern cathedrals, the gathering
places for urban populations and amongst the grandest buildings
of their age. 'We are no longer the men of cathedrals and
meeting halls, but of grand hotels, railway stations, vast
highways, colossal harbours...', wrote Sant'Elia, anticipating
an age of perpetual motion.

At the same time, however, the railways were the means
whereby the dense populations of the 19th-century city could be
dispersed - Welwyn Garden City in Hertfordshire would have been
inconceivable without its rail link to London. Railways spawned
suburbia and the dispersal of urban humanity was vastly
encouraged by the development of the motor car. In Los Angeles,
the world saw the first great city in which the car was a prime
mover (even Los Angeles had its origins as a significant city
in a mass transit system - now being revived). The post-1945
era saw American and, increasingly, European cities transformed
to meet the needs of a mass car-owning public. Brussels and
Birmingham were surrounded by a tight girdle of motorways.
In many countries, most obviously the USA, rail travel declined
rapidly - New York's Penn Station was a victim of the decline,
not because its commuter numbers fell but because the railways
were no longer a prestige industry, needing landmark premises.
Air travel took the prime chunk of the business, yet the airport
could not be an urban building type. As airports grew, indeed,
they moved further and further out of the cities, so that
Tokyo's Narita, New York's JFK and London's Heathrow were
a tortuous remove from the centres they served. The great
airports became cities in their own right, huge employers,
generators of massive incomes, symbols of a new society
in which traditional cities were obsolete.

The 'energy crisis' of the 1970s was the beginning of
a reassessment of the role of transport in the environment.
Slowly, rail systems got new investment, new lines were

constructed, passenger numbers grew as road congestion
increased. Transport began to be seen not just as a means
of moving people but as an engine of regeneration. In Paris
the Météor metro line and in London the Jubilee Line Extension
absorbed the lessons of Hong Kong - where a metro system was
built from scratch in little more than a decade - and applied
them to previously undeveloped, rundown quarters. In Bilbao,
the new metro paved the way for the renaissance which gained
world recognition only with the opening of the high-profile Gehry
Guggenheim Museum. Having built the metro, Bilbao moved forward
to looking at the integration of all its transit systems in one
central interchange - at the beginning of 2000, the vision was
yet to be realized.

Hong Kong, the city that had discovered mass transit
systems in the 1970s, led the way at the end of the 20th
century in demonstrating how a transport system needs to be
seen holistically. Chek Lap Kok airport is not simply a major
intercontinental hub. From the start, it was conceived as a link
in a chain. Kowloon Station was the next link, the place where
the international traveller joined a national and local transit
system - Terry Farrell's idea of 'urbanizing the airport'
is no mere fancy. As Heathrow, JFK and other formerly isolated
airports are joined to the cities they serve by fast transit
links, the airport terminal becomes an urban building type,
a stage in a progression from city centre check-in to boarding.
As airports are joined to surface transport systems that may
be the gateway to a whole continent, they are no longer
cities apart.

At a time of dynamic change, it is reassuring to know that
the great stations of the past are not redundant. New York's
Penn Station and Grand Central, Roma Termini and Florence's
Sta Maria Novella, and the great central stations of Frankfurt,
Stuttgart and Hamburg are being reconfigured as focal points
for the city and urban gateways - no longer are they merely the
end of the line.

BILBAO
New metro and
Abando transport
interchange

(1988-   )

The remarkable success story of Bilbao – from declining rustbelt city to focus of tourism and culture in two decades – has produced a world-class landmark in Frank Gehry's acclaimed Guggenheim Museum. Yet the renaissance of Bilbao is founded not on isolated monuments but on an integrated development strategy that stresses the importance of infrastructure to the regeneration process.

Politically marginalized during the Franco years, Bilbao nonetheless retained its economic significance and sense of identity, though the fabric of the city suffered from ill-considered development and the steady growth of traffic. Given its confined and elongated site, squeezed between hills along the river Nervion, Bilbao faced strangulation by the car. The economic boom of the 1980s put more pressure on the transport system, so that city, provincial and regional governments, given a new degree of autonomy from Madrid, resolved to develop the public transport network and to construct a new metro. By the mid-Eighties, planning and consultation exercises were well advanced and an international competition for the design of the metro was held in 1988, with Norman Foster the winner. Construction work began in 1990 and the first phase of the system – eleven stations – opened in 1995, with work on further phases still continuing. With a total length of 61 kilometres (38 miles) the Bilbao metro utilizes existing lines beyond the city centre, which is crossed by a tunnel cut into the rock. The essence of the system is generous scale – big tunnels and wide trains – and Foster's stations are a far remove from the claustrophobic passageways of the London Underground (in its pre-Jubilee Line Extension incarnation). The stations are formed within 100 metre- (328 foot-) long, 16 metre- (52 foot-) wide 'caverns', tall enough for the ticket halls to be suspended within them. Lined with pre-cast concrete cladding, these spaces are immensely dignified. With a strictly limited palette of materials – concrete, glass and steel, classic graphics by the late Otl Aicher – and a complete absence of the customary clutter of

left
The site of Bilbao,
squeezed in along a
river valley between
mountains, has posed
problems for the
city's development
since the 1960s, when
traffic began to
strangle its centre.

right
The metro system,
constructed from 1990
onwards, utilizes
existing lines
outside the city
centre, which is
traversed by a tunnel
cut through rock.

right
The aim of Foster's
competition-winning
scheme was to
integrate the new
metro stations into
the streets and
squares of the city.

left, top and bottom
Sarriko is unusual
amongst the new metro
stations in being a
freestanding
building in the
townscape.

right
The interiors of the
stations are generous
in scale, with ticket
halls suspended
within the tunnels.

advertising and slot machines, the stations are also a reassertion of the importance of public transport in the modern city. For Foster, they also hint at the excitement and poetry of movement. The stations make their mark on the city streets, where the characteristic glazed 'Fosteritos' have become a familiar site – a reinterpretation, perhaps, of the famous Guimard Paris Metro canopies of the 1900s. Great care was taken with the siting of the Fosteritos, so that they are integrated into the streets rather than intruded. Beyond the station entrance, there is in every case a clear, largely daylit route through to the trains. Deceptively light in appearance, but made for long use and

A striking new bridge
designed by Santiago
Calatrava is another
of the landmarks of
the new Bilbao.

hard wear, the Bilbao metro applies the lessons of Foster's larger transport buildings to the streets of an historic city, enhancing them in the process.

The as yet unrealized Abando interchange, designed by Michael Wilford & Partners and having its origins in a project designed by Wilford with James Stirling in the 1980s, equally addresses urban as much as purely transport issues. The existing Abando terminal stands close to the river, at the point where the medieval core of Bilbao meets the 19th- and 20th-century city. The effect of the station, with its flanking sidings and sheds, is to create a solid, elevated mass which overshadows nearby streets and blocks any circulation across the site – the building is, in every sense, a terminal, a dead end. The reconstruction project turns the site into a lively interchange, not only for local and intercity trains, but also for buses and the metro. The new complex is to be part of the city, not a place set aside for those in transit. It can be entered by pedestrians from all sides and at several levels. The excitement of rail travel is rekindled in a great glazed shed covering a public plaza, a great urban room with a roofspan twice that of London's St Pancras station and containing shops and restaurants. A World Trade Centre, offices, apartments and a hotel are ranged around the concourse – a total of over 300,000 square metres (3.2 million square feet) of space. The sheer scale and ambition of the project has hindered its realization, and substantial modifications are possible, but the Abando site remains a problem which Bilbao must at some stage resolve as part of the next stage of its ongoing regeneration.

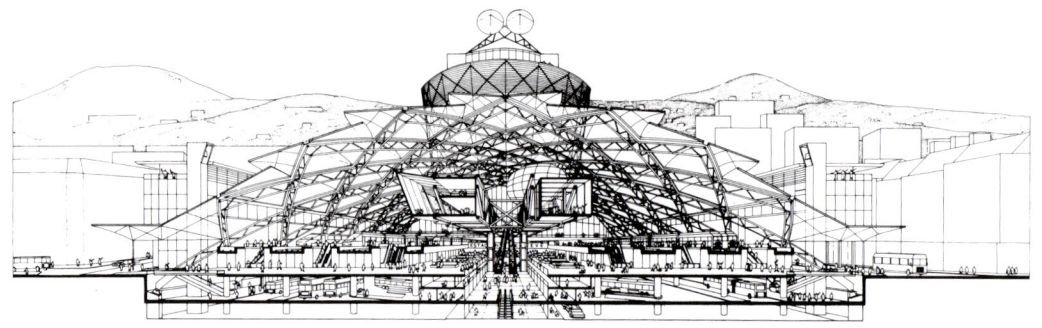

Michael Wilford's
reconstruction of the
Abando rail terminal
transforms a 19th-
century station
into an integrated
transport interchange
and improves links
across the city.

The Bilbao
Guggenheim, designed
by Frank Gehry, has
become one of the
best-loved buildings
of the 20th century
and is the flagship of
Bilbao's campaign of
regeneration. The
museum's appearance
changes dramatically
as daylight turns
to night.

STUTTGART
Station quarter/
Avenue 21

(1993-2020)

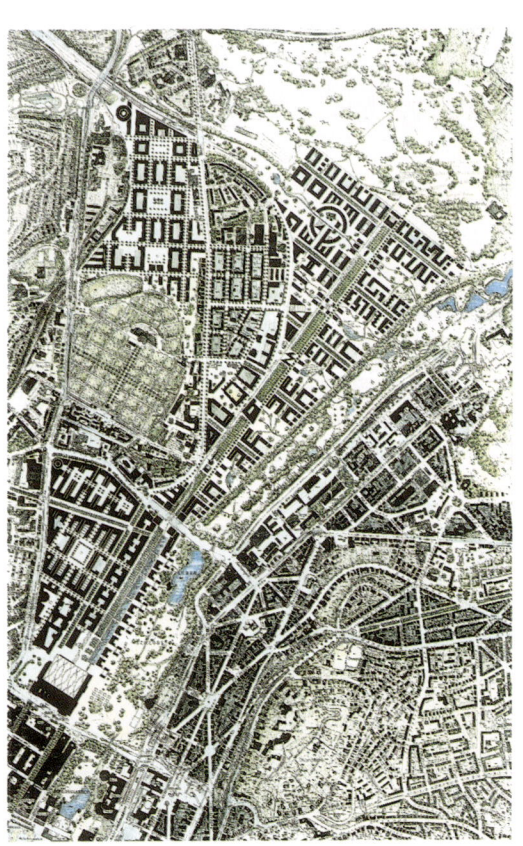

Von Gerkan Marg's project for the reconstruction of the central station in Stuttgart exemplifies the degree to which improved transport links and the development of a high-speed European rail network are acting as catalysts for change in many old-established European cities. The existing Hauptbahnhof in Stuttgart is a classic of its period, begun (to designs by Paul Bonatz and F.F. Scholer) in 1911, though not completed until 1928. The architectural vocabulary of the building, like that of New York's Grand Central, is monumentally Classical, though at Stuttgart the usual decorative embellishments are omitted to produce a composition which impresses by virtue of its composition and disposition of abstract masses. Despite its central location, the station is close to areas of parkland (typical of the city), notably the gardens of the historic Schloss. As usual, however, the mass of tracks and marshalling yards serving the station forms a great gash in the fabric of the city, severing one district from another.

The starting point of the scheme is the redesign of the station to reflect changing perceptions of rail travel – von Gerkan Marg, for example, is involved in the design of the new generation of high-speed trains. Since Stuttgart is no longer to be a terminus, but a through station, the present layout is obsolete. The existing platforms become redundant. The tracks are depressed by 14 metres (45 feet), and realigned at right angles to the original station building, to create a site of around 100 hectares (250 acres) for redevelopment. A new glazed concourse building, with daylight flowing right down to the platform level, is linked to the refurbished Bonatz concourse, which is seen as a visible 'gateway' to the city for outsiders and a gateway to the new development area for everyone – rather than, as at present, an end-stop to the city centre. Architecturally, the counterpoise of the original building – heavy and even severe – and the lightweight, glazed intervention promises to be exciting.

The central element of von Gerkan Marg's masterplan is the Avenue 21 – a 2.2 kilometre-

Stuttgart aims to create a new city quarter over the tracks leading into its early 20th-century Hauptbahnhof (bottom centre of main picture) – itself to be transformed as part of Germany's new high speed rail system.

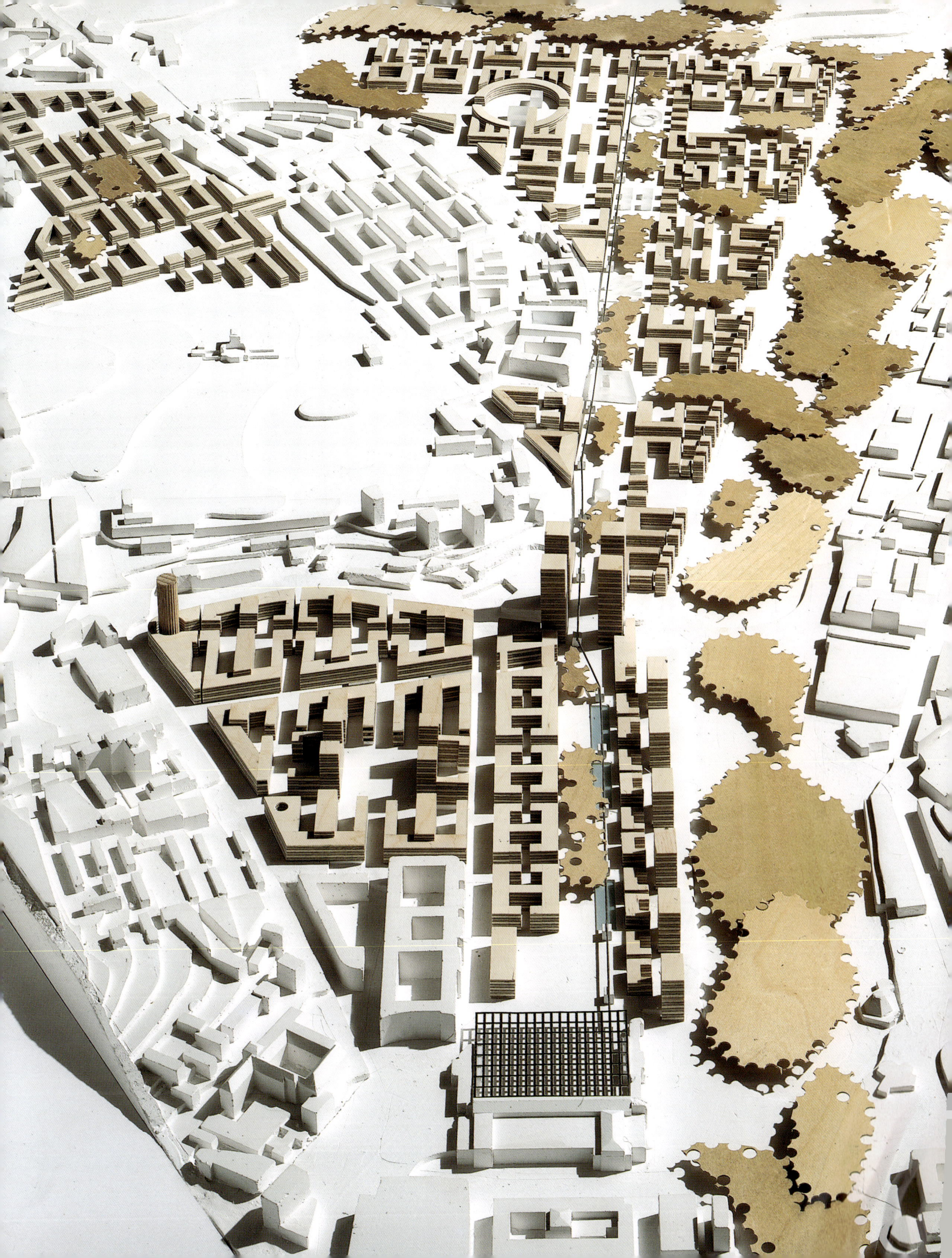

S
U

BÜROS
LADEN
MAGNETBAHN
EINGANG
LADEN
ICE

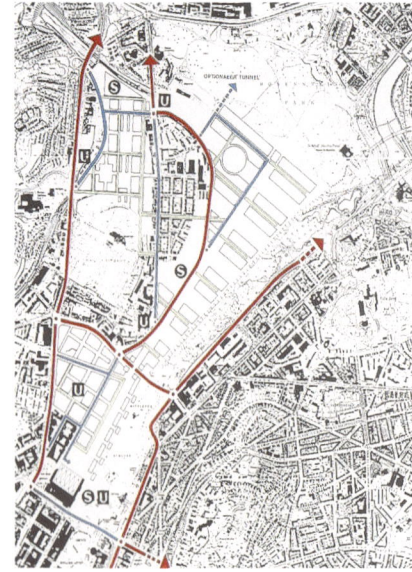

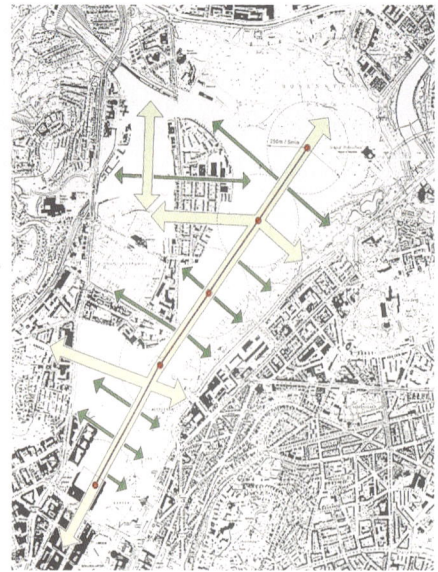

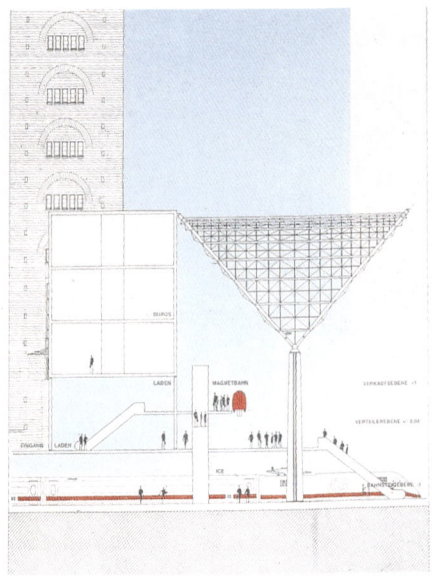

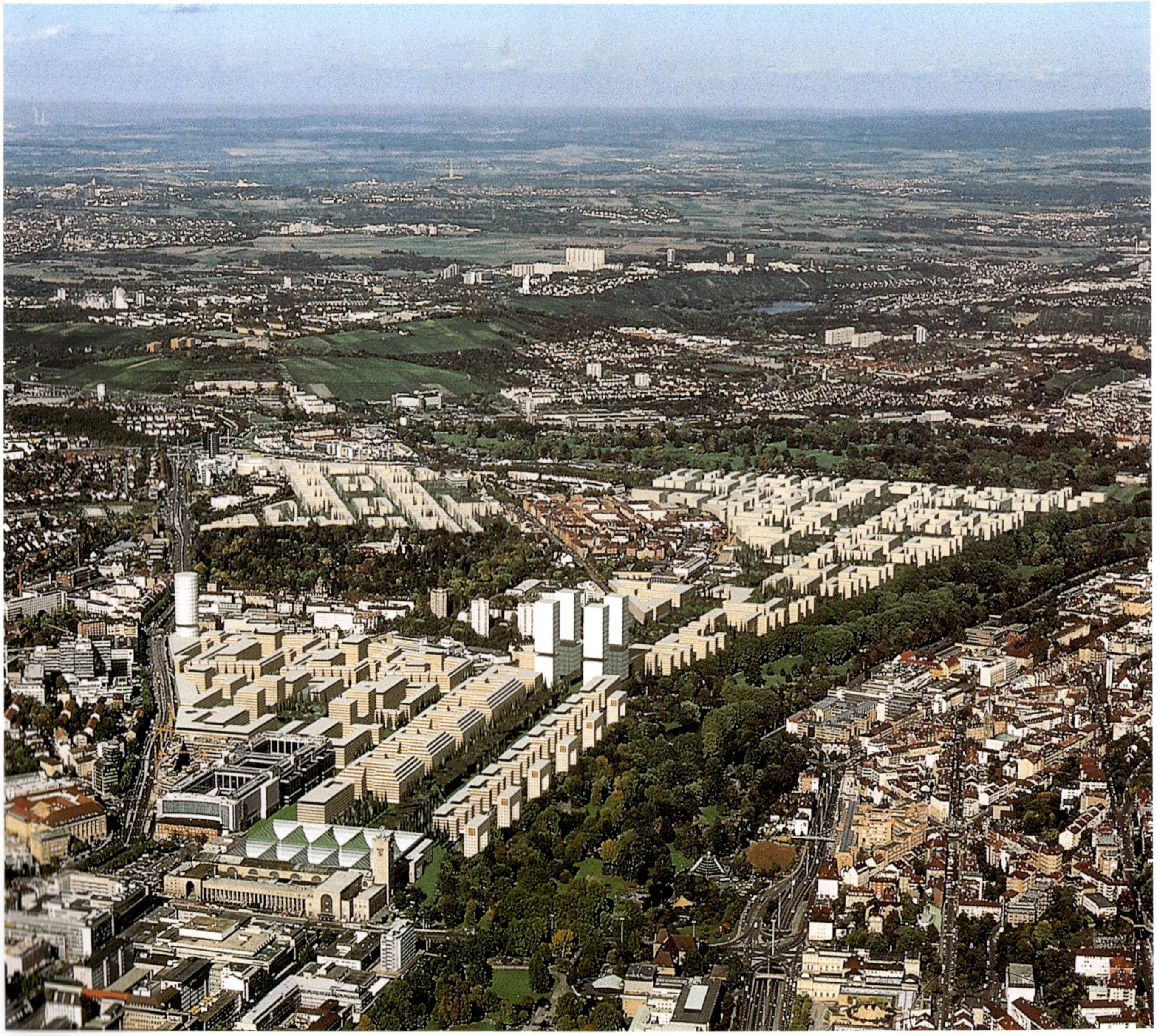

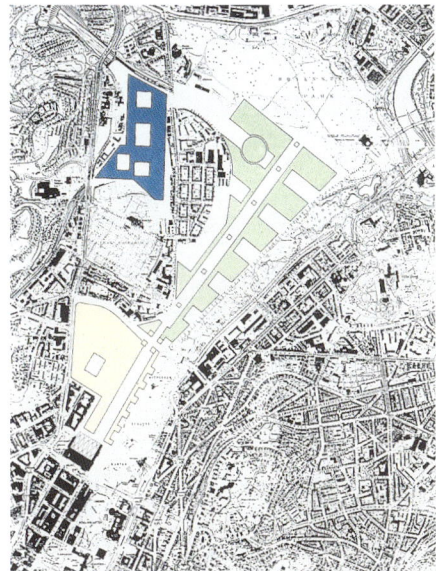
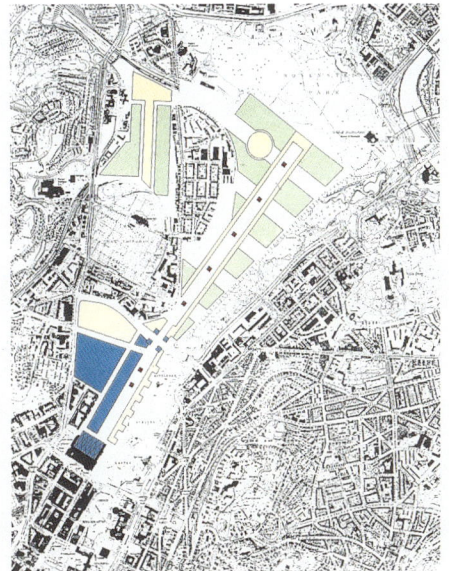
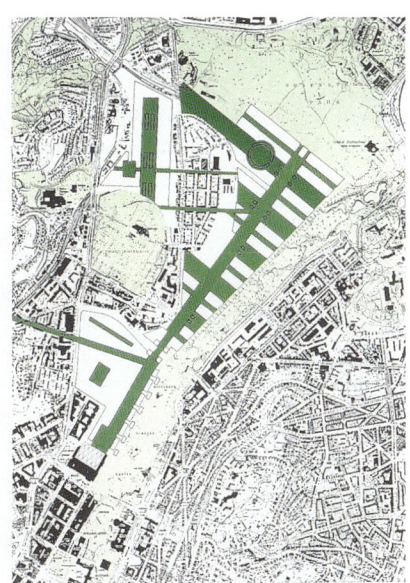

top left, top right and above
The phased development of the new city district replaces a chasm of rail tracks and marshalling yards with workplaces and homes in a green, but urban, setting.

left
The new quarter is focussed on a linear park lined by office and residential blocks - a rapid transit system provides fast access to the further parts of the development.

(1 $^{1}/_{3}$ mile-) long, 70 metre- (230 foot-) wide public space which runs from the station to the existing Rosenstein Park – a reincarnation of New York's Park Avenue, but greener and linked to a commitment to mixed-use development. The avenue is intended principally for pedestrians and a monorail (the Magnetbahn) is proposed to provide a fast link from one end of the site to the other. Along its length, the avenue is diverse in character, with residential and commercial quarters and a marked shift from a formal urban layout to a more park-like form as it joins the Rosenstein Park. Around the station, the task is one of urban repair, reusing existing buildings and filling in the gaps left by the reconfiguration of the station. The form of the development lends itself to phasing – the project is seen as reaching over several decades.

A natural corollary of the project is the linking of areas of the city that have traditionally been divided by the railway – bold new cross-city connections are established and as a result the tendency towards social stratification is challenged.

The Hauptbahnhof is
to be transformed
from a terminus into a
through station. Von
Gerkan Marg's
reconstruction
respects the landmark
terminal of 1911-28
while adding to it in
a contrasting,
lightweight manner.

HONG KONG
Chek Lap Kok
airport,
Kowloon station

(1989-   )

Hong Kong is sometimes claimed as the archetypal late 20th-century city, a place of perpetual motion and perpetual, virtually untrammelled change. A product of British colonialism, Hong Kong has welcomed successive waves of immigrants since the conversion of mainland China to communism in 1949. In 1997 the colony was subsumed into China, but its dynamic individualism appears to have survived the take-over. An element in that individualism, perhaps, is Hong Kong's disregard for conventional notions of urban design – at densities of up to 80,000 to a square kilometre, it is argued, normal planning orthodoxies are irrelevant. Hong Kong is, notwithstanding its chaotic form and the squalid living conditions of many of its inhabitants, a worldly success – a fact underlined with satisfaction by determinist critics. Hong Kong has generated very little architecture that addresses anything beyond commercial criteria – Foster's Hong Kong Bank remains a notable exception. So does 'good' architecture really matter (cynics might argue) when it comes to creating a successful economy?

It is easy, however, to exaggerate the element of the unplanned and the ugly in Hong Kong. During the 1970s and 1980s, for example, the metro system (43 kilometres/27 miles long, with 38 stations on three lines) was built from scratch, the first section opening in 1979. It now carries more passengers than the London Underground. The last years of British rule saw the inauguration of a group of linked infrastructure projects which would have equal significance for Hong Kong's future in an increasingly competitive Asia where Hong Kong's economic hegemony was being challenged by Seoul and Shanghai, Bangkok and Ho Chi Minh City. Significantly, these projects produced architecture of world quality – the Bank no longer stood alone.

Proposals for a new airport to replace the long inadequate Kai Tak were mooted in the early 1980s, but not until 1989 was the island site at Chek Lap Kok, 23 kilometres (14 miles)

離港
Departures ↗

詢問處
Information

接機大堂
Arrivals hall

餐廳及商店
Restaurants, Shops

洗手間
Toilets

In the vast atrium of Chek Lap Kok, incoming and outgoing passengers are placed on different levels, but all can enjoy the exhilarating grace of the architecture.

from the centre of Hong Kong Island, identified as the site. Chek Lap Kok, a small island of 300 hectares (740 acres), was to be quadrupled in size, by means of land reclamation, to accommodate one of the world's greatest airports, and linked to Kowloon and Hong Kong Island by fast road and rail connections. Five years of work was needed to complete the dredging and earth-moving operations. A masterplan for the airport layout was published in 1991 and formed the basis for a competitive tender exercise to secure designs for the terminal – the winner, Mott Consortium, included Foster & Partners (alongside Mott Connell Ltd and BAA plc), and Foster's stamp is clearly apparent in the architecture of the 1.3 kilometre- ($^4/_5$ mile-) long terminal. The project is a development of Foster's acclaimed – but far smaller – Stansted (London) terminal, with services and baggage handling consigned to basement level and, in this case, two levels of passenger handling above. As at Stansted, masterly use of natural light is a key element in the design. The strongly directional form of the terminal is expressed in the system of 129 circular section steel shells (spanning 36 metres/118 feet) on a diagonal grid, forming barrel vaults running from east to west. Passengers enter and leave the building through the vast atrium, with departing passengers passing on glass bridges over the heads of those arriving. There can be few more exhilarating points of entry to any country.

Chek Lap Kok opened in 1998. In the same year, Hong Kong completed one of the world's greatest railway stations in West Kowloon, part of the transport network which forms the backbone of a new linear city. The Chek Lap Kok project was seen not simply as an out-of-town airport, but as a component in a new approach to air travel – Terry Farrell, architect of the Kowloon Station, sees it as a matter of 'urbanizing the airport'. Check-in either at Hong Kong Station (much expanded by Arup Associates) or West Kowloon is fundamental to the concept – the airport is a 20-minute train ride away. At West Kowloon, the airport trains

connect with the Hong Kong metro system and
with mainline services. The station was also the
nucleus for a new 1 million-square-metre (11
million-square-foot) Kowloon 'super city' built
on reclaimed land, with a series of landmark,
40-storey towers challenging those across the
water in Hong Kong and alleviating the
monotony of the existing Kowloon landscape of
high-rise apartment blocks.

Farrell's station had the luxury – hitherto
unknown in the Hong Kong region – of a huge
empty site, nearly 14 hectares (35 acres) in size.
The station is slotted into a concrete 'box', 300
metres (980 feet) long, 180 metres (590 feet)
wide, up to 18 metres (58 feet) deep, sunk into
the sandy, waterlogged ground. Trains are
located on two subterranean levels, with the
metro in tunnels below, so that there was no
pretext for the lightweight, glass and steel
aesthetic familiar from 19th-century stations
(and recalled in recent station projects by, for
example, Nicholas Grimshaw and von Gerkan
Marg). Kowloon Station is unapologetically
heavyweight and solid, carved out of the
foundations of the city above, as it were, with a
succession of contrasting monumental halls –
the concourses serving each level of the station
– to give a sense of direction and place. Solidity
is not a matter of aesthetic preference but of
structural necessity – the huge columns are
designed to carry the weight of the
developments on top of the station and transfer
them down to the bedrock below. The grid of
the station was to dictate the grid of the new
city above. Only in the centre of the complex,
where the passenger enters from Station Square,
does an element of lightness emerge – the core
of the station is to remain free of 'air rights'
developments, a light-filled place of intense
movement, of comings and goings, where the
everyday life of the city meets the drama of
international travel and all the layers of the
station are connected to each other and to the
city above. Air travellers are marshalled, here as
at the airport itself, into arrivals and departures
on opposite sides of the tracks – an odd
resuscitation of the system which applied in

Terry Farrell's
Kowloon Station
(below and bottom) is
the interchange point
for passengers
arriving from the
airport, with
connections to
mainline and metro
services. It occupies
a reclaimed site and
is engineered to
carry a massive
superstructure of
office towers (right).

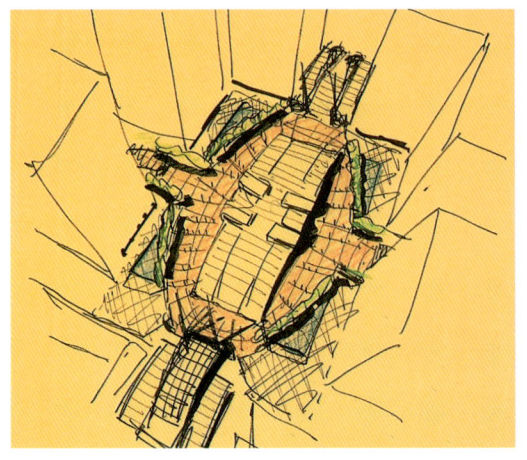

Farrell has set his
mark on Hong Kong,
with the Peak Tower
(left) and the
monumental and
colourful
Ventilation Building
which serves Kowloon
Station (right, top
and bottom).

The new Hong Kong
metro system has
produced impressive,
spacious stations,
designed for large
numbers of passengers
- this is one of the
busiest systems in
the world.

Victorian termini such as London's King's Cross and Paddington, but clearly practically necessary in the light of estimated passenger flows (up to 3,500 hourly leaving the station, half of them by taxi).

Farrell's ability to inject drama into purely functional requirements is demonstrated in the Kowloon Ventilation Building, which stands close to the station. The building is designed to sit in a future park and has deliberately been given a striking form. Farrell has written of the project: 'The organic design... is based on an undulating form relating to both rolling landscape and the waves of the adjacent harbour'. The towers of the building contain a ventilating plant for the underground rail tracks.

Terry Farrell's remarkable run of projects in Hong Kong (including the prestigious new consulate and British Council headquarters) includes the Peak Tower, on one level part of the transport system (it is the terminus for the funicular railway serving the Peak), but equally an unashamed attempt to create a new landmark and visitor attraction, with shops and restaurants to supplement the spectacular views. Farrell, as much as anyone, believes in the referential and narrative role of architecture to create a sense of place and identity. The Peak Tower is a real landmark, in a city that needs markers of this kind.

九龍
Kowloon

Farrell's Kowloon Station combines a clear, multi-level diagram with a monumental quality found in few recent railway buildings.

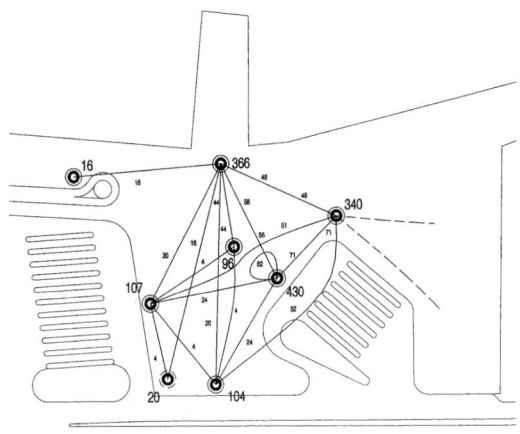

ARNHEM
Arnhem Central

(1997-   )

The Arnhem Central project builds on the existing significance of the Central Station (used by 65,000 daily) as the epicentre of the Dutch city of Arnhem to create a new and dynamic heart for this growing centre, where transport systems are linked to workplaces and new homes. Designed by UN Studio/van Berkel & Bos, the project includes 74,000 square metres (800,000 square feet) of offices, 10,000 square metres (110,000 square feet) of retail space, 1,000 parking spaces, 150 apartments, a new bus station and an extended and improved rail station – not to mention parking for 5,000 bicycles. A collaboration between central and local government, the EU and private developers, Arnhem Central is designed to be constructed in phases over a decade or more.

Bus and rail facilities are combined in a new multi-level interchange, climate-controlled and providing access to all parts of the development. The development, say the architects, is about movement – 'movement studies are therefore the cornerstone of the proposal: the analysis of the types of movement on location includes the directions of the various trajectories, their prominence in relation to other forms of transportation on the site, duration, links to different programmes, and interconnections'. It is the analysis of movement that determines the form of the development – 'surveys as to waiting times and transfer percentages are used to identify spots suitable for the creation of secondary programmes, such as fun shopping and run shopping. The intersection of different traffic systems is reduced to a minimum to optimize pedestrian accessibility to all the facilities.' This ethos of providing fast and easy transport links that also take into account human needs can be seen as the way forward in city centre regeneration for the 21st century.

UN Studio/van Berkel & Bos's Arnhem Central masterplan focuses on the existing main railway station of the city, turning it into an integrated transport hub, a place of movement, arrival and departure, which is linked to a new urban landscape connected to the old city centre.

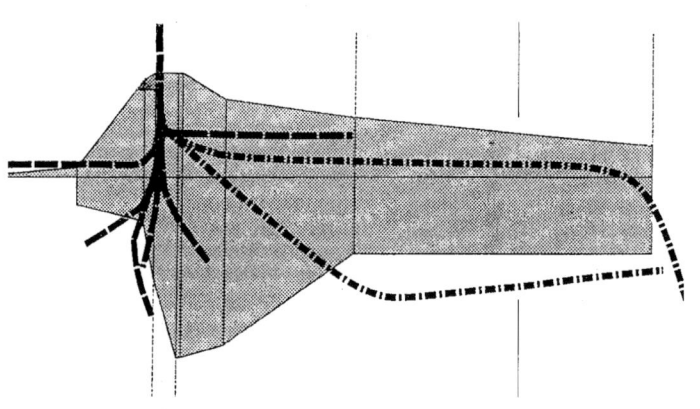

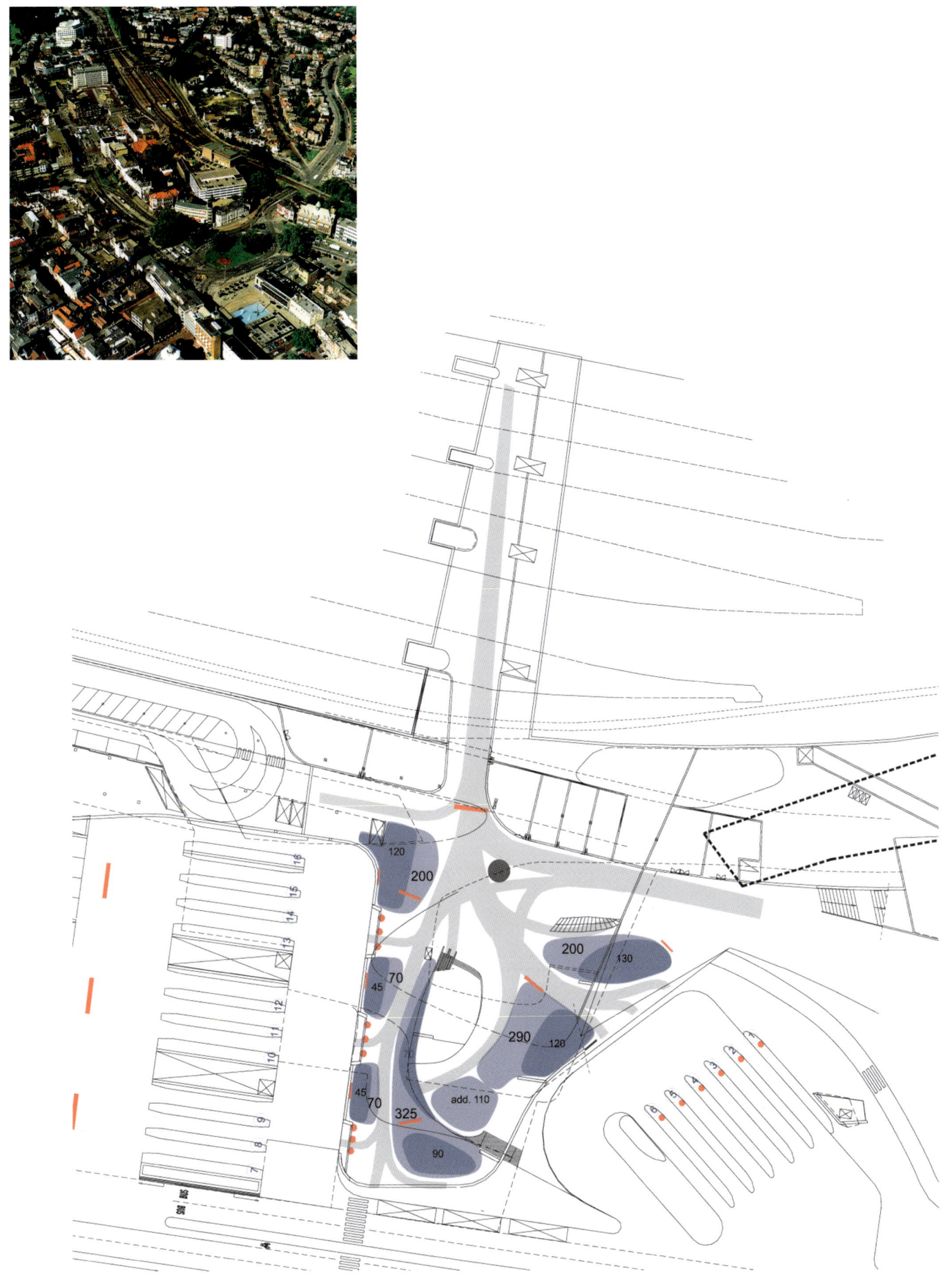

The form of the
development is rooted
in ideas of movement
and connection - the
flexibility of the
plan allows for
the detailed
configuration of
buildings to be
decided as the
programme evolves.

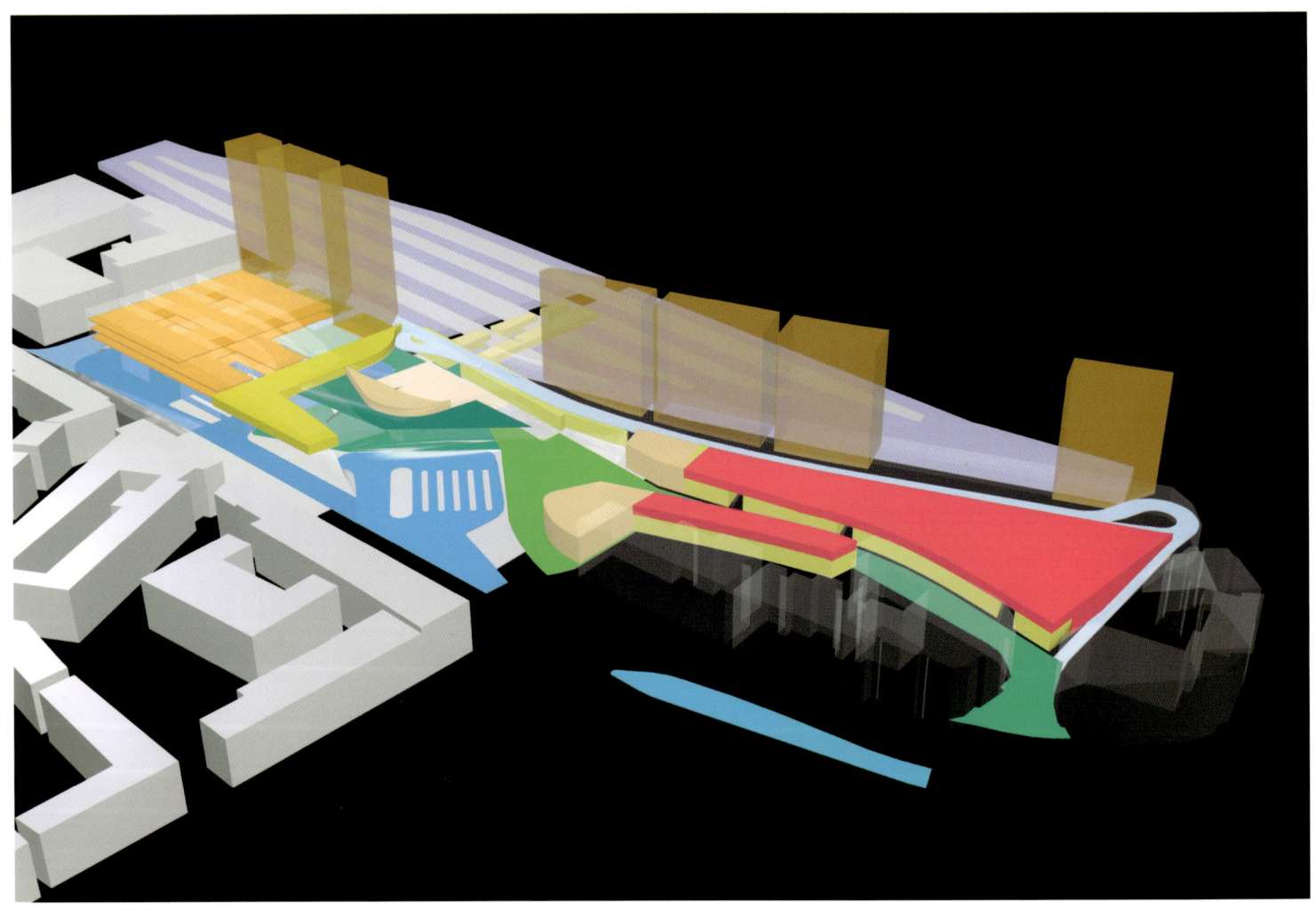

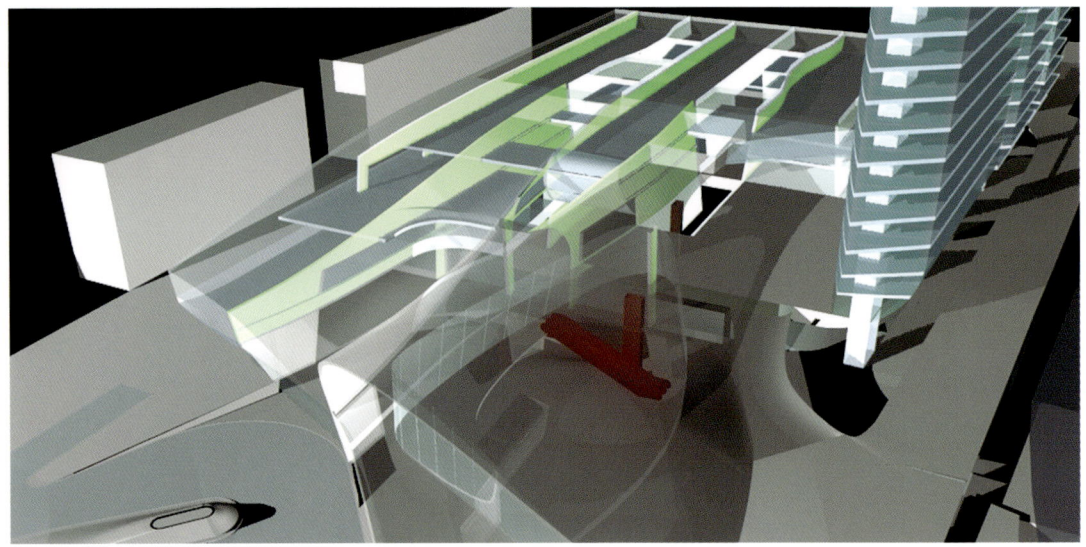

The completed development will be an intense megastructure containing shops, housing, parking and public transport facilities. The layering of the project reflects intensive studies into the diverse and sometimes conflicting needs of a wide range of users.

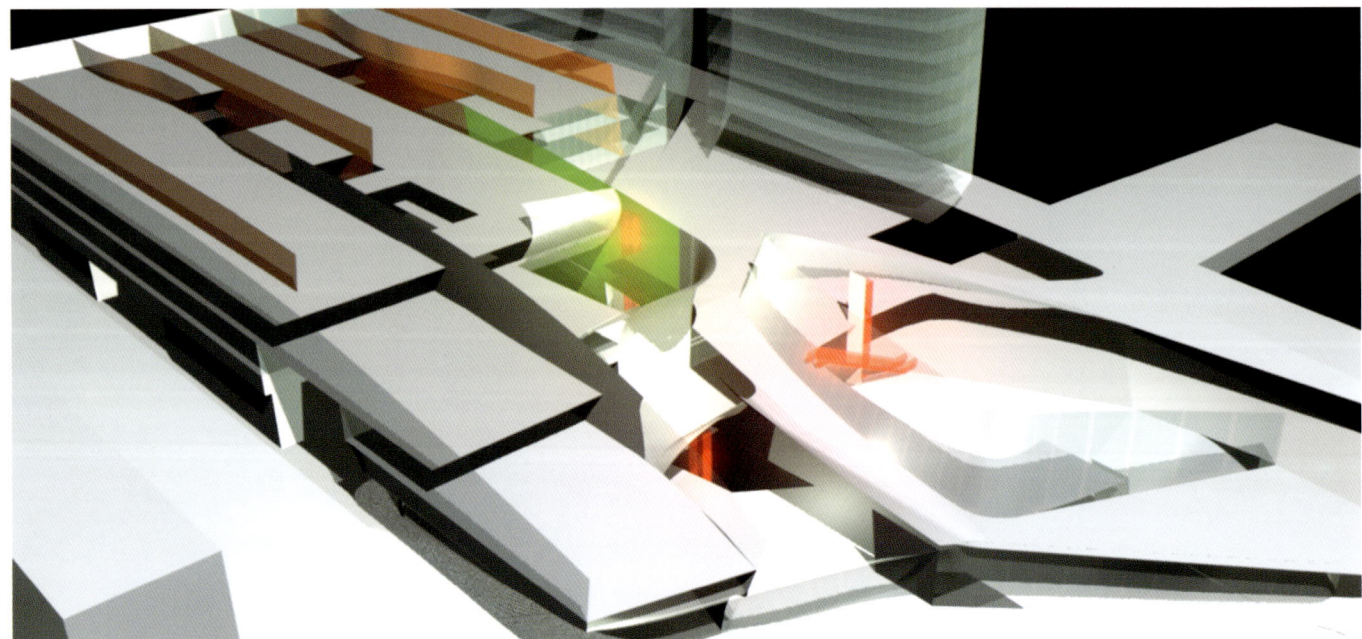

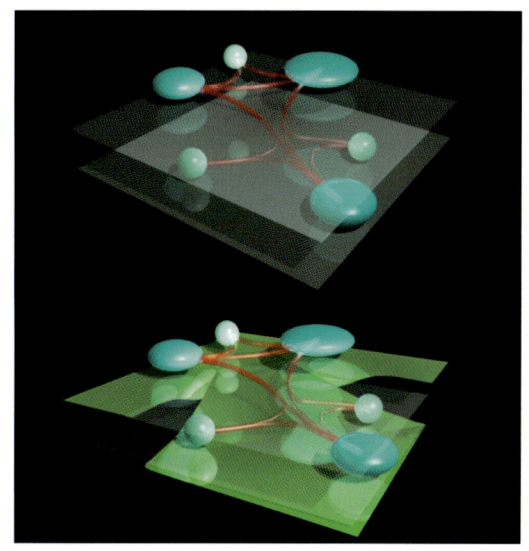

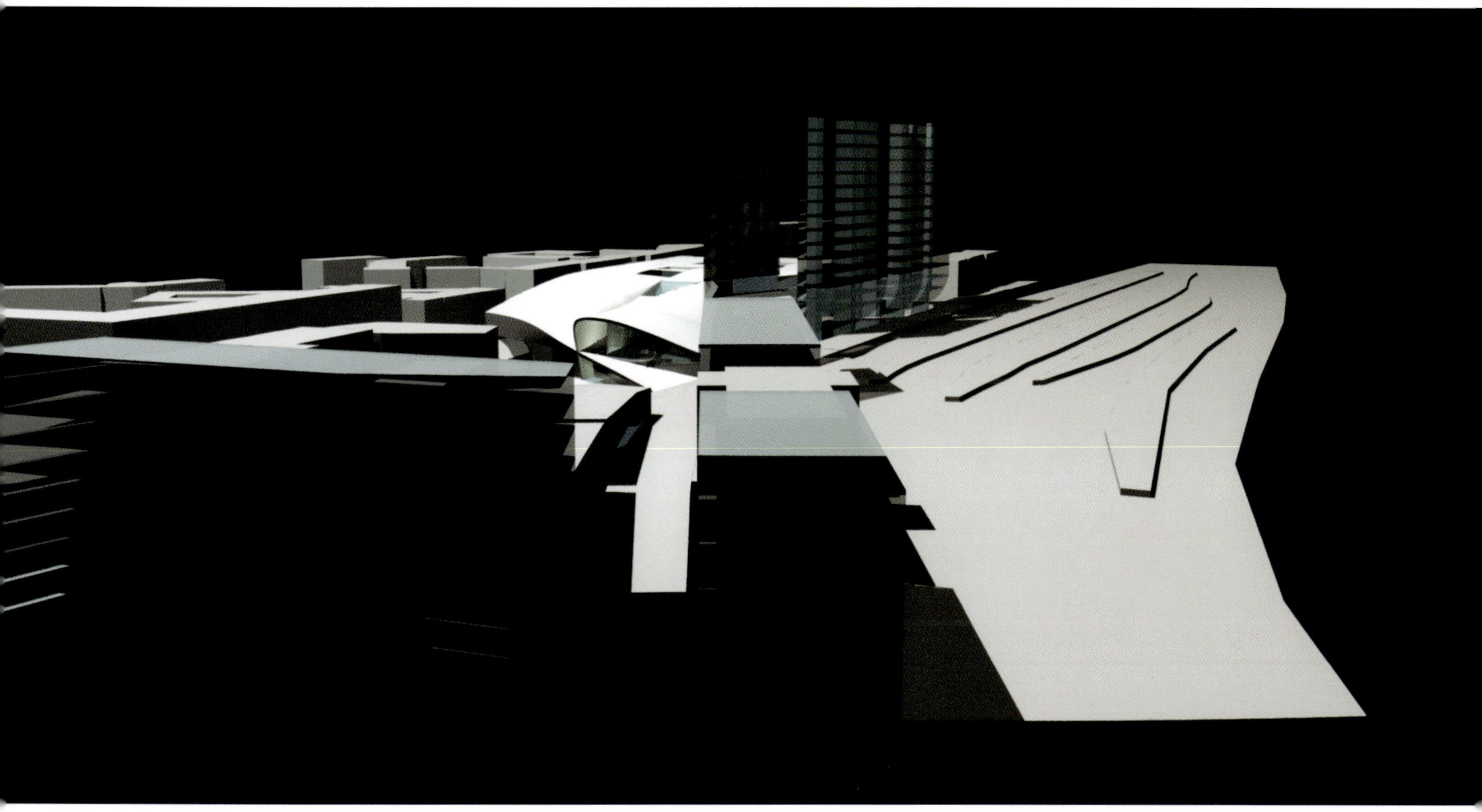

FRANKFURT AM MAIN
Station quarter/ Frankfurt 21

(1996-   )

In Frankfurt, as in Stuttgart, von Gerkan Marg's masterplan for the area around the Hauptbahnof combines a radical restructuring of rail facilities with a bold attempt to repair the damage done in the past by the incursions of the railway into the city.

Frankfurt's main station is one of the grandest in Europe, with three huge arched iron and glass sheds (completed in 1888) symbolizing the three railway companies that were united there – a symbol of the new united Germany of the Kaisers. Prefacing the sheds, G.P. Eggert's concourse building is itself a powerful symbol of the power of the 19th-century railway, with a great central arched window expressing the trainshed behind. The station was damaged in the Second World War, but faithfully restored. A few blocks away stands a major freight station, served by a further tangle of rail tracks and yards.

Eggert's concourse block and trainsheds are valued historic structures and the architects faced the challenge of integrating them into a recast through station, with tracks sunk 20 metres (66 feet) below the streets. The concourse building is retained intact and remains the main point of entry to the station. The sheds remain unchanged, but now cover a deep galleried space extending down to the tracks – three levels of galleried walkways, containing two kilometres ($1^1/_4$ miles) of shop fronts, not only give a powerful character to the transformed interior but equally act as a structural grid for supporting the weight of the iron roofs. This bold move is in the spirit of 19th-century railway engineering – augmented by the new technical possibilities available in the 21st century.

The freight station is to be completely demolished and replaced by an underground facility. This produces around 70 hectares (170 acres) of development land, with almost as much land secured from the redevelopment of the main station. The freight station adjoins the Frankfurter Messe, one of the largest trade fair facilities in Europe. A new Messeboulevard will be laid out on the site, a planted pedestrian

The reconstruction of Frankfurt's Hauptbahnhof is linked to an ambitious plan for a new mixed-use district on reclaimed railway lands.

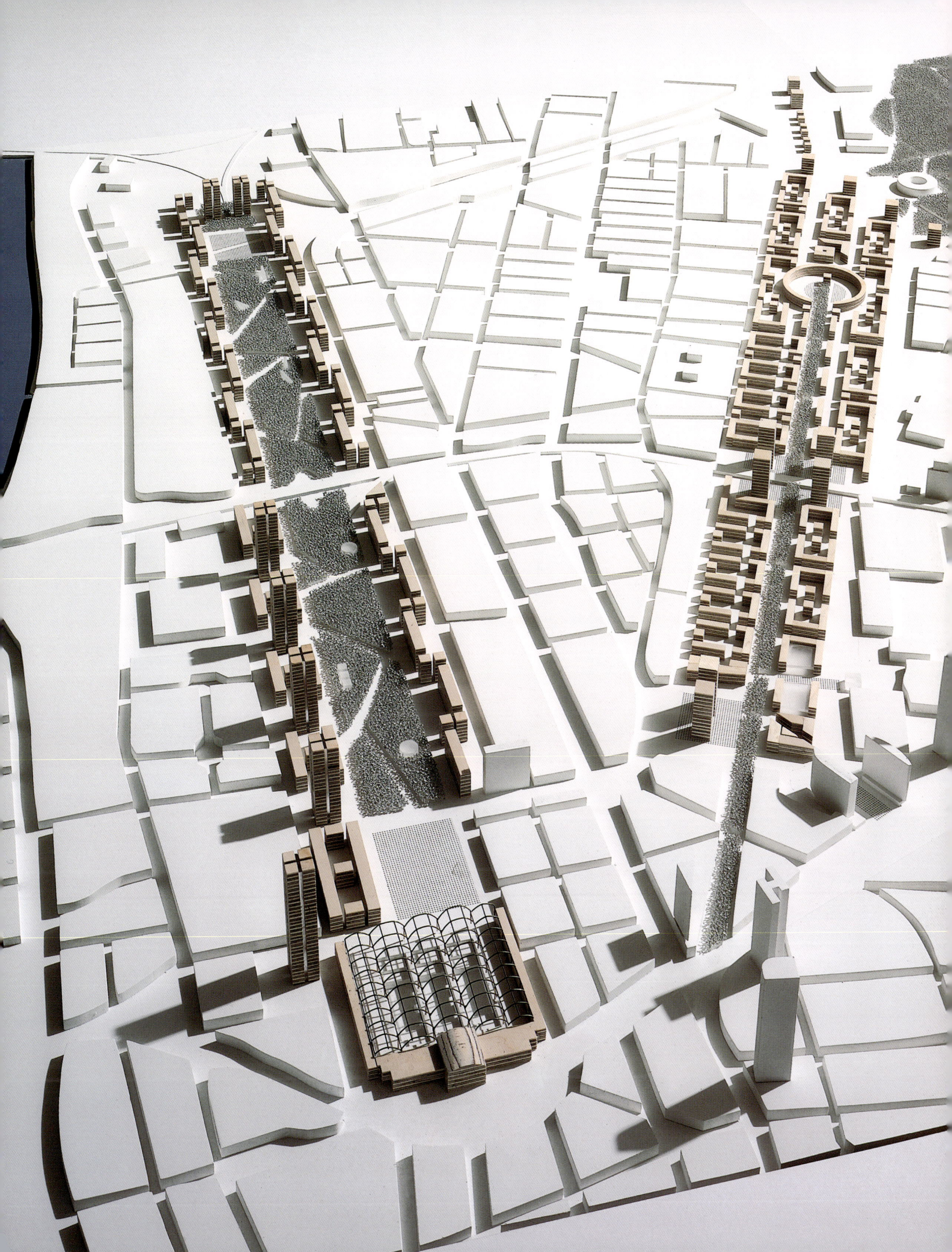

The existing tangle of tracks (below) serving the great passenger terminal and the nearby freight depot will give way to a new park and areas of offices and housing (left).

route, modelled on Barcelona's Ramblas, with trees and water and bordered with new office and residential blocks. Beyond the Hauptbahnhof, a new 'central park', 3 kilometres ($1^4/_5$ miles) long, with lavish planting in an explicitly romantic manner, will form the focal point for a new mixed-use district of the city. Dense housing development is balanced by two dramatic high-rise office towers – part of Frankfurt's bid to increase its hold on Europe's financial industries.

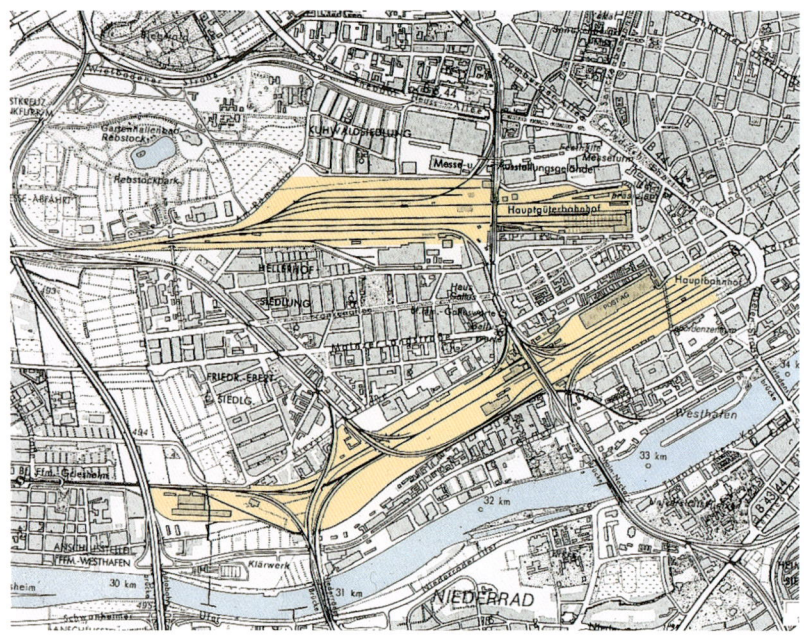

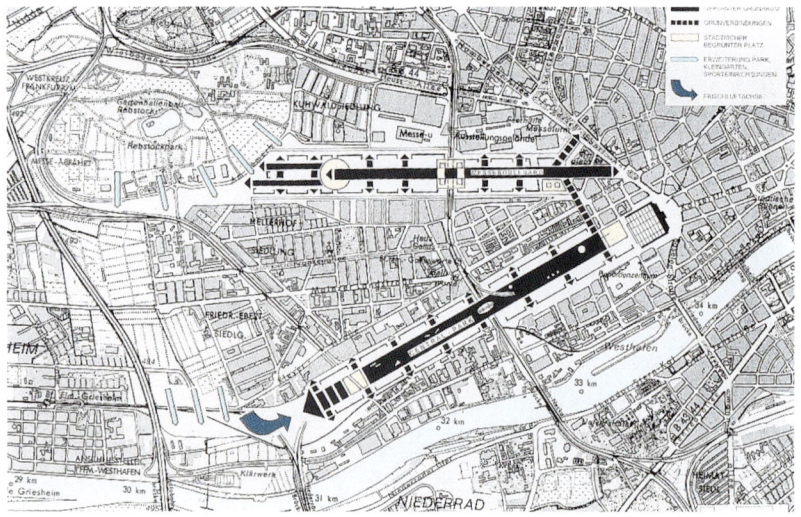

left
The station has always been a point of arrival and an end-stop to the city centre – phased plans show how it now becomes the gateway to the new city district constructed 'over the tracks'.

right
The great 19th-century train sheds are retained and shops and restaurants are slotted in along galleries above the tracks – now sunk below ground as part of a radical restructuring of the system.

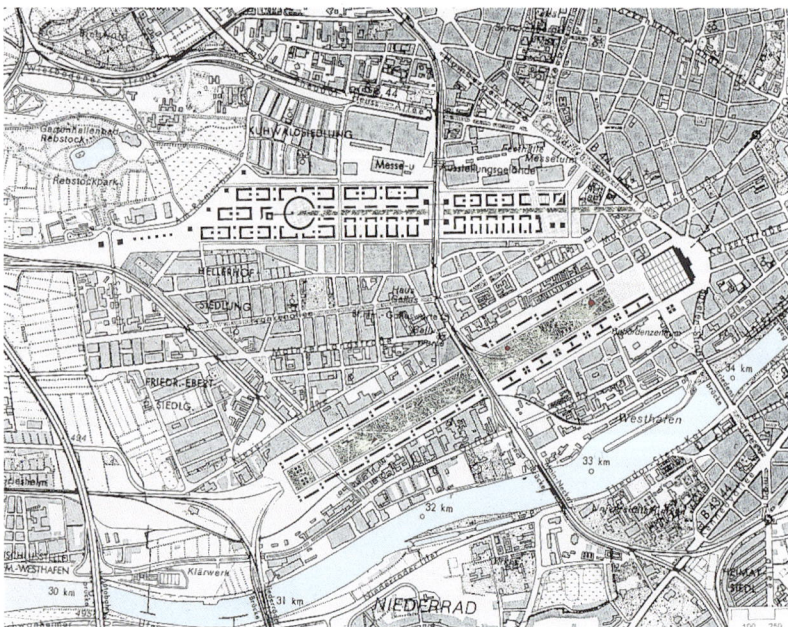

Culture
and
the
City

Investing in culture is a surefire route to urban regeneration. The fact that art pays was confirmed in the 1990s with the huge success of Frank Gehry's Guggenheim Museum in the Basque city of Bilbao. In its first year of opening, the Guggenheim attracted 1,350,000 visitors, including a large number from outside Spain. Previously seen as an unprepossessing industrial city, Bilbao became a tourist destination. The Museum generated $100 million in revenue for the city. In one year, in fact, it repaid its construction cost (which had been borne by city, regional and provincial governments). Since the contents of the Guggenheim are on loan from the foundation of the same name, future returns will be net profits for Bilbao.

Bilbao's cultural renaissance is striking, but pales beside that of Barcelona, where the Museum of Contemporary Art designed by Richard Meier in the previously squalid Raval district is just one of a number of major investments in the arts which have added lustre to what was always a cultured and cosmopolitan city. Placing major arts buildings in rundown neighbourhoods is a proven way of attracting investment. Paris turned Beaubourg around in the 1970s, with the construction of Rogers and Piano's Pompidou Centre, cementing the revival of the adjacent Marais. In London, the opening of the Tate Modern in the former Bankside Power station, on the 'wrong' side of the Thames, has already made this part of Southwark a tourist zone and small galleries, loft-style apartments and restaurants are colonizing under-used buildings. Covent Garden became the most visited area in London after the famous fruit and vegetable market quit in the early 1970s and specialist shops, bars and restaurants moved in – the renovated central market building became the focus of the neighbourhood. The completion (in 1999) of the Royal Opera House reconstruction project – begun in the mid-Eighties – confirms Covent Garden's position as a centre for the performing arts. But the ROH development is also a good example of urban repair, filling previously vacant sites and restoring the historic Floral Hall (another market building), with public access to many parts of the new complex. The traditional notion of theatres and concert halls being open only to those who buy tickets is fast fading.

The urban cultural revolution has revolutionized the way that 'culture' itself is defined. The Dutch city of Groningen set out to build a new museum in a defiantly anti-elitist spirit, actually encouraging passers-by to take short cuts through the building and to go there for entertainment as much as enlightenment. The rationale was that many people were intimidated by old-style museums, but might be attracted by works of art, archaeology and antiquity shown in a novel way. So the new museum became not a monument, but a chunk of city fabric, with a number of architects contributing (surprisingly diverse) elements to one of the most extraordinary arts buildings of the late 20th century. The spirit of Groningen is far removed, for example, from that of the Getty Museum in Los Angeles. Trumpeted as the key museum of the 1990s, the Getty suffers from its self-imposed isolation, like a hill town, a latter-day Xanadu cut off from city life.

Nor does 'culture' mean simply the traditional 'high' arts. The alternative culture of night club and bar provides a more subversive but equally effective means to renew cities. More than 30 years ago, the first 'lofts' were established in redundant factories and warehouses in New York's SoHo, challenging zoning laws (so that planners stipulated initially that only artists might inhabit them). A new housing form was established. Whole districts were brought back from dereliction and the redevelopment machine was halted.

The most fundamental quality of the successful 21st-century city is diversity – of form, activity and humanity. The arts have never fitted into narrow planning definitions. They will continue to play a key role in forming the liveable cities of the future.

LONDON
Royal Opera House
Reconstruction

(1983-99)

There has been a theatre at the heart of Covent Garden since the early 17th century, though the Royal Opera House as an institution has existed only since 1946. It occupies the imposing theatre built to designs by E.M. Barry in 1857–8, after an earlier structure designed by Robert Smirke was destroyed by fire. The ROH is one of the most famous venues for opera and ballet in the world.

Not designed with the needs of its present users in mind, Barry's theatre proved steadily more inadequate in terms not only of technical specification but equally of audience comfort and amenities for performers and other staff. Many facilities, including rehearsal studios and scenery storage, had to be outhoused far from the ROH. The removal of the historic fruit and vegetable market from Covent Garden to south London in the early Seventies provided an opportunity for the ROH to expand its constricted site and a substantial extension was completed in 1982. The continuing failings of the house led, however, to a competition the following year in which Jeremy Dixon and William Jack were selected to develop a scheme of reconstruction and extension. The project was subsequently developed, with the involvement of Edward Jones, by Dixon Jones: BDP and was completed, after long delays, at the end of 1999 following a three-year construction period.

The ceding to the ROH, by the government of the day, of cleared land around the theatre provided scope for development, though at least one historic structure, the iron and glass Floral Hall (intended as a winter garden for opera goers but later downgraded for market use) had to be incorporated. Under the Thatcher administration, it was made clear that no further subventions would come from the public sector and that a commercial approach to development would be necessary. The first scheme for the site incorporated substantial areas of commercial office and residential space, in line with the booming property market of 1980s London. Criticism of the scheme from community groups and others led to a .

The reconstructed Royal Opera House occupies an entire city block, containing the historic theatre and large new rehearsal and backstage areas, as well as generous public spaces

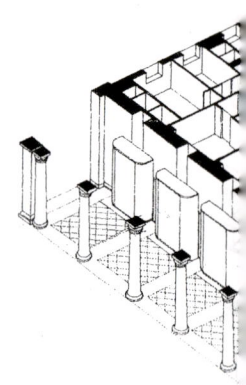

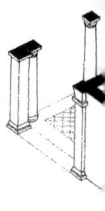

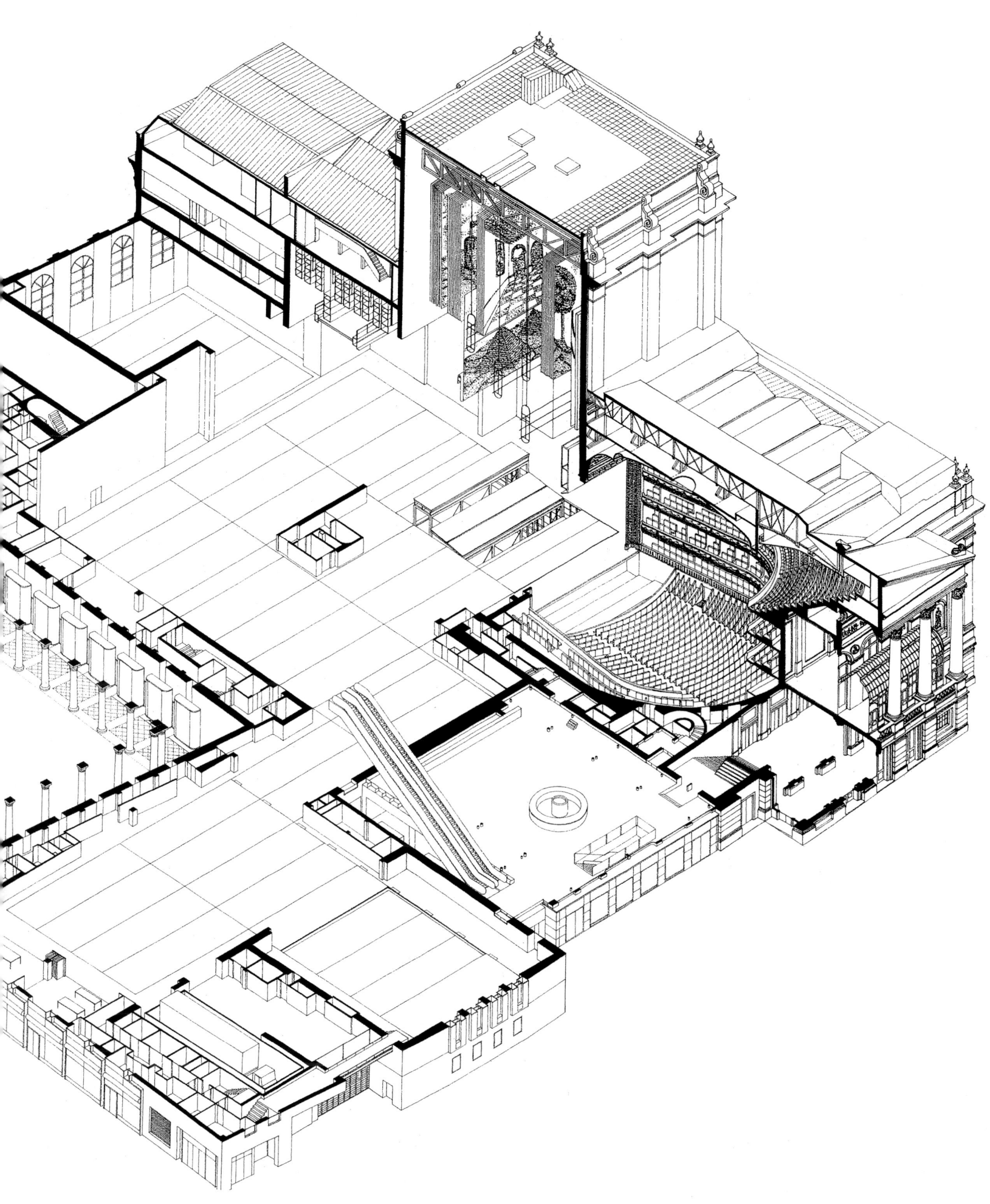

The reconstruction of part of the long-lost piazza was a fundamental part of the project from the start - shops at ground level complement the adjacent market.

progressive revision – helped by the recession of the early 1990s – whereby the commercial elements were removed and the entire development given over to ROH use. A major grant from the newly inaugurated National Lottery, plus generous support by private benefactors, made this change of direction possible. Stage, back of house and rehearsal facilities are now as good as those in any of the other great opera houses of the world. Audience amenities have improved immeasurably. The restored Floral Hall, with its long-lost barrel vault reinstated, provides a gathering place for audiences. Those sitting at amphitheatre level previously suffered from the worst facilities, but now enjoy a large bar area with access to external loggias overlooking the Covent Garden piazza. Escalators provide rapid communication between all levels of the house. The Barry auditorium has been little altered (and there are only 80 extra seats), but the installation of air conditioning is a boon for audiences.

The restoration of
the 19th-century
Floral Hall as a
public space adjacent
to the Victorian
opera house was
another key idea in
the project, in which
urban repair was a
prime objective.

right
New staff facilities
include a rooftop
canteen with terrace.

below
Once obliged to
travel to and from
far-flung areas of
suburban London,
performers now enjoy
modern on-site
rehearsal spaces.

The essence of the scheme, in terms of its urban design concept, has altered relatively little since 1983. The original piazza blocks by Inigo Jones had long vanished, but had been partially reconstructed in the 19th century. It seemed an obvious move that the reinstatement of the piazza elevations should continue. This has been achieved, however, not as pastiche or replica, but as a reinterpretation of the Classical tradition, using natural stone and reviving Jones's Italianate device of an arcaded ground floor. From the arcade, there is direct access from the piazza to all parts of the ROH – Barry had deleted the piazza entrance which was a feature of the earlier theatres on the site.

The redeveloped ROH is not just a building, but an entire city block and it is appropriate that the architectural language of the project is diverse – on Russell Street and James Street, the aesthetic is uncompromisingly modern, with open jointed cladding and boldly formed metalwork. On Bow Street, the individual elements in the scheme form an undeniably picturesque composition.

The entire scheme represents a delicate balance between conservation and redevelopment, between history and modernity – but, the architects argue, this balance is basic to all successful cities, where a regard for the past does not exclude a concern for present and future needs. As such, it is probably unique in Britain and provides a powerful riposte to the still dominant high-tech approach of Foster, Rogers and others. Some critiques of the scheme have focussed on stylistic issues, raising the (largely irrelevant) issue of post-Modernism. But the core of the project is its concern for public space and for allowing the public domain to permeate what was, in the past, a closed and private world. The underlying rationale of this approach – both financial and political – is clear, but it has given London a dimension previously lacking and challenged architectural and planning orthodoxies. It is hard to imagine a more vivid example of culture reshaping the city.

The centrepiece of
the scheme is the
restored interior of
E.M.Barry's opera
house, one of the most
famous theatres in
the world.

PARIS
Seine Rive-Gauche

(1991-2010)

Dominique Perrault's Bibliothèque Nationale de France is one of the most ambitious and extraordinary of the *grands projets* initiated under the Presidency of François Mitterrand. The outcome of an international competition held in 1989 and completed in 1996, the Library has been criticized for the supposed illogicality and impracticality of its diagram, with books stored in glazed towers at the four corners of a vast rectangular block, containing the toplit reading rooms. Perrault set out, however, to design not simply a library, but a new Parisian landmark, 'a hybrid of temple and supermarket', with a great garden at its heart. Moreover, the *très grande bibliothèque* is not an isolated monument, oddly consigned to the fringes of central Paris, but a key element in a strategy of regeneration and renewal.

Eastern Paris (like the East End of London) has never been affluent or fashionable. In the 19th century, it became heavily industrialized along both sides of the river Seine. On the left bank, the hinterland of the Gare d'Austerlitz developed from the mid-19th century onwards as an area of railway yards, factories and warehouses, a sharp contrast to the elegance of the Jardin des Plantes, west of the station. In the years after the Second World War, this quarter of the 13th arrondissement steadily declined as old industries waned and the SNCF (France's national railway) rationalized and modernized its operations, making traditional marshalling yards redundant.

The regeneration of eastern Paris advanced steadily during the Mitterrand era, with the opening of the new Finance Ministry at Bercy (for civil servants transplanted from the Louvre), the adjacent Parc de Bercy and the Palais Omnisports arena. The process of renewal shifted across the Seine in the 1990s with the initiation of the Seine Rive-Gauche masterplan. Approved by the city authorities in 1990–91, the plan envisaged new housing, offices and public spaces on the redundant industrial lands beyond the Gare d'Austerlitz. The concerted development zone (ZAC) designated at that time covered 130 hectares (320 acres) – nearly a

The site for the Seine
Rive-Gauche project
is close to the heart
of Paris but, like
much of the east end
of the capital, was
blighted by 19th-
century railway and
industrial
development.

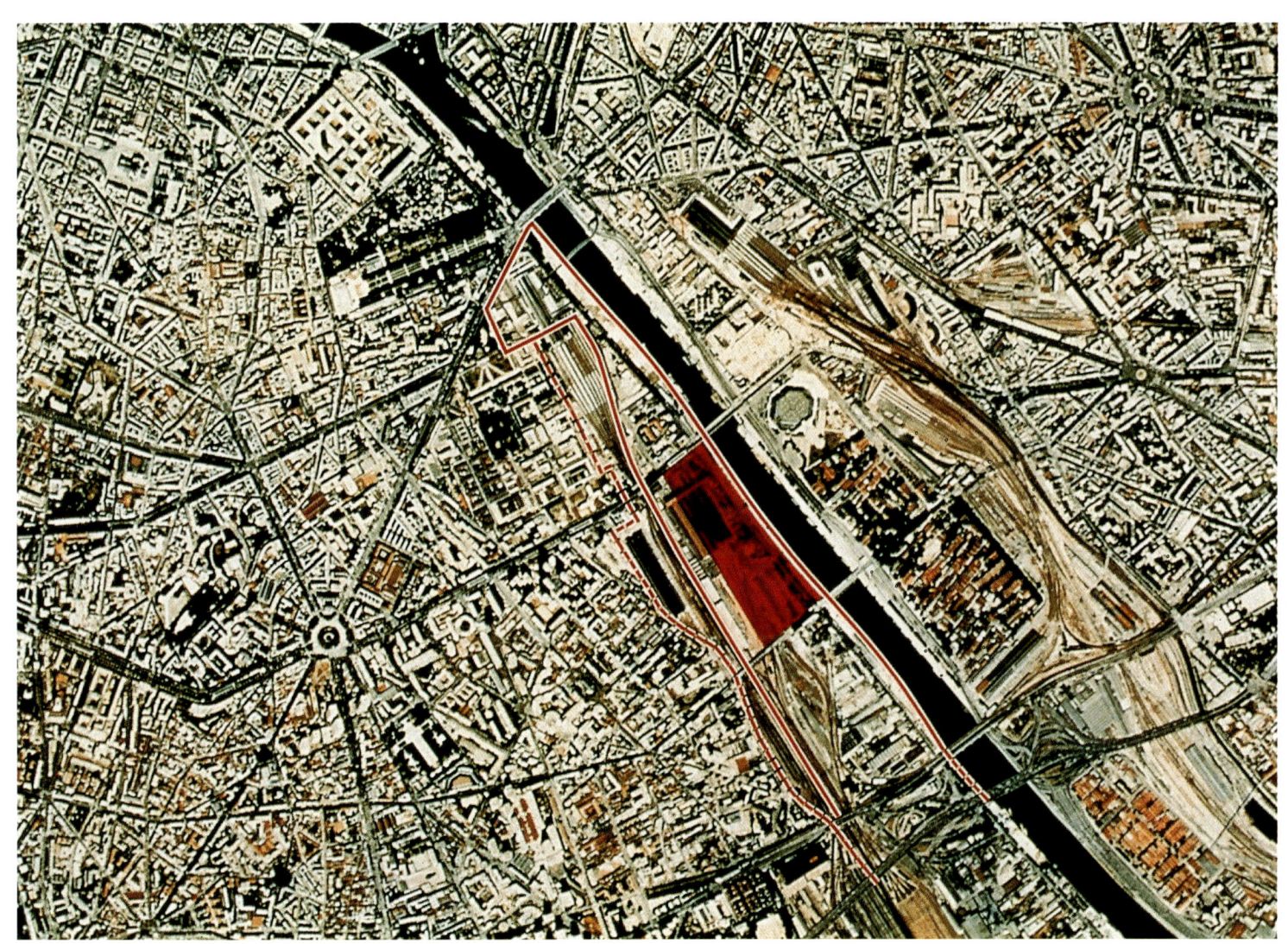

fifth of the total area of the 13th arrondissement
– along the riverside. Although traditionally
detached from the life of the capital, this
quarter had many natural assets, including good
road and public transport links (with metro and
RER lines). Two main rail termini, Austerlitz and
the Gare de Lyon (just across the river), were
close at hand. Post-war planning policy in Paris
had strictly limited office development within
the historic core – hence the growth of the
office city of La Defense west of the centre. New
office buildings were rare in central Paris and
there was a concern that major national and
international companies, unable to find the
accommodation they needed, would shun the
city. Seine Rive-Gauche offered great potential
for addressing their requirements, but the stress
from the start was on an area of mixed use. The
masterplan provided for 900,000 square metres
(9.7 million square feet) of offices, employing
up to 60,000 people, but also for 5000
apartments with a residential population of up
to 20,000 – the housing provision, moreover,
would span the range from 'luxury' to
subsidized social units. Traditional and new
industries and crafts were to be provided for
with 150,000 square metres (1.6 million square
feet) of space. Local shopping was to be
provided, along with schools, public libraries
and parks. Most strikingly, the total area of
public space was to exceed 300,000 square
metres (3.2 million square feet).

The implementation of the project has been
delegated to SEMAPA, an agency in which the
city is the majority shareholder and which had
developed the masterplan with APUR (the
Atelier Parisien d'Urbanisme). A fundamental
feature of Seine Rive-Gauche was an emphasis
on infrastructure provision as a first priority. A
new Seine bridge, named after Charles de
Gaulle, a direct link to the Gare de Lyon, was
opened in 1997 and was followed by a new
footbridge. The new Météor metro line, which
serves the Bibliothèque Nationale, was
completed in 1998. The spine of the new
quarter is the 40 metre- (130 foot-) wide
Avenue de France, sitting on top of the rail

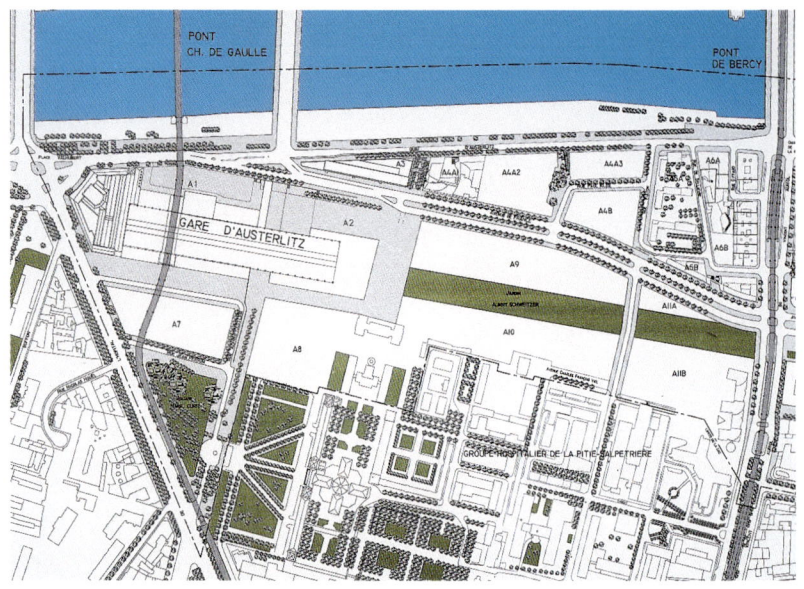

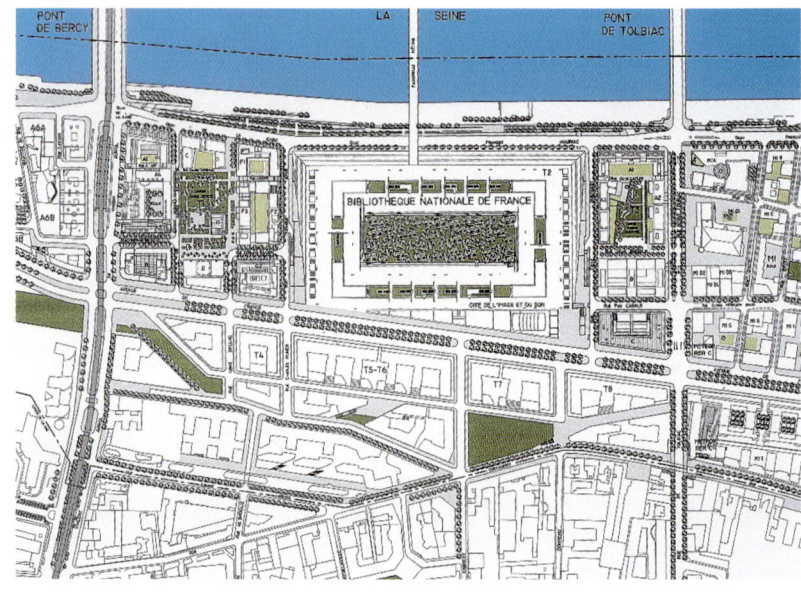

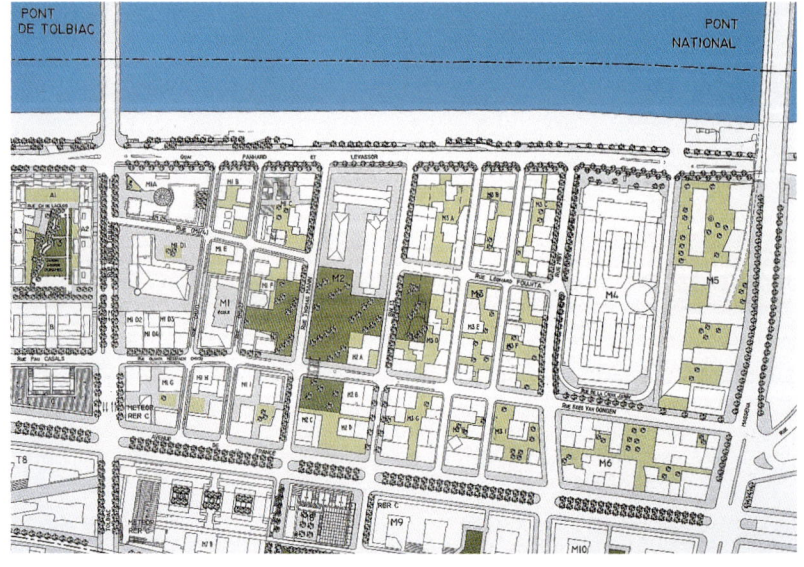

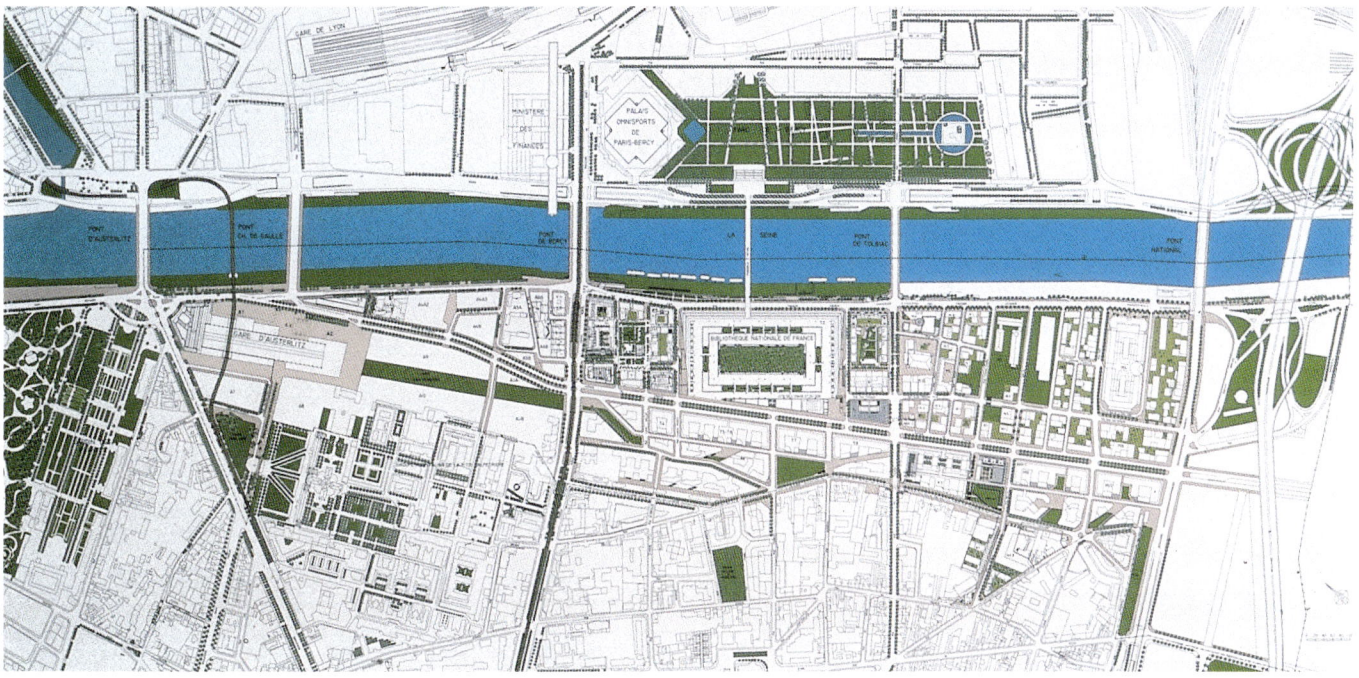

left
The masterplan for
Seine Rive-Gauche
focusses on a great
new avenue in the
tradition of
Haussmann's
boulevards.

above and below
New road and metro
connections were
fundamental to the
project, breaking
down the isolation of
the hinterland of the
Gare d'Austerlitz.

overleaf
Dominique Perrault's
four-towered
Bibliothèque
Nationale is a
monumental presence
on the Left Bank and
spearheaded the
regeneration of the
surrounding area.

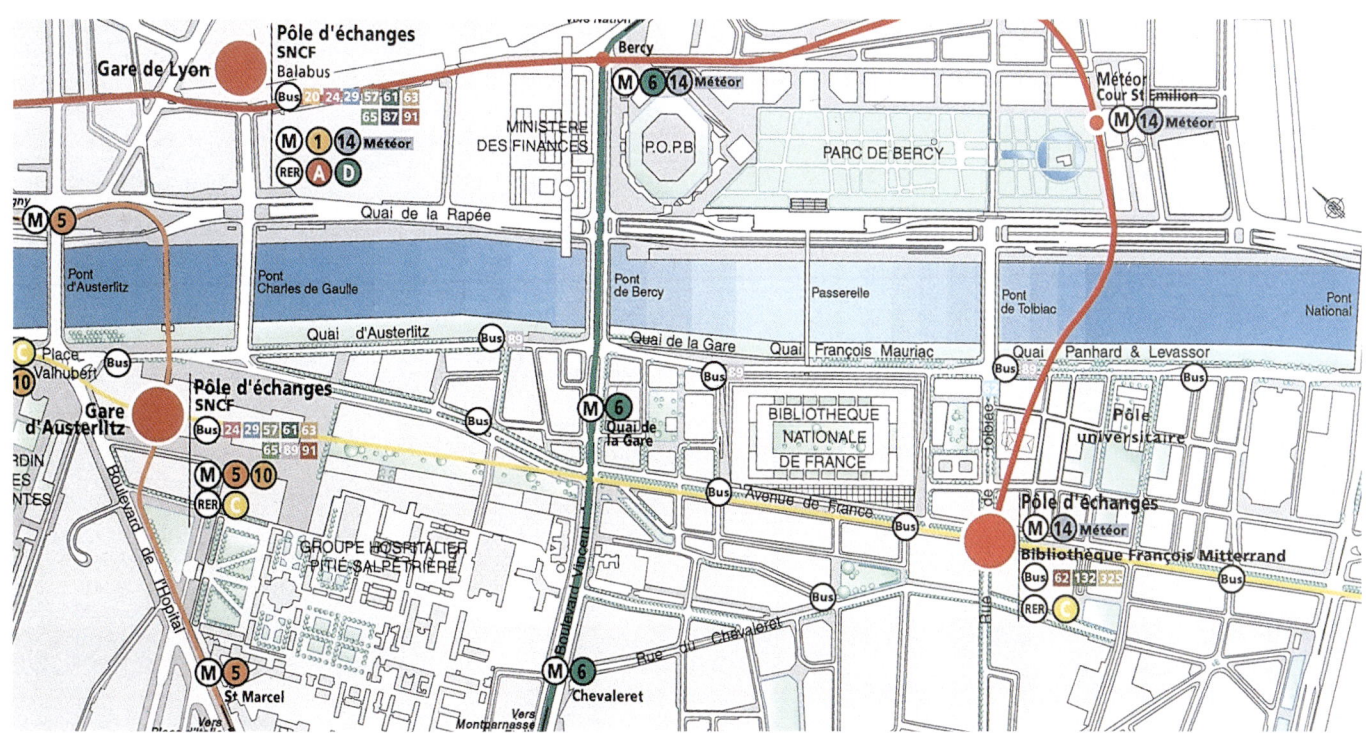

left
The Charles de Gaulle bridge was built in 1997 to link the Gare d'Austerlitz on the left bank with the Gare de Lyon (the tower of which can be seen in the centre of the picture) on the right bank.

below
The new Bibliothèque Nationale complex includes a footbridge across the Seine.

right
The new architecture of Seine Rive-Gauche is in a broadly modern tradition – blocks address traditional streets.

Culture and the City

tracks into the Gare d'Austerlitz, a civilized thoroughfare in the tradition of the 19th-century boulevards, with broad, tree-shaded pavements, a natural habitat for cafés and restaurants to serve office workers and customers in the new stores lining the avenue.

The development of Seine Rive-Gauche has been broken down into three major neighbourhoods – Austerlitz, located around the station and historic Saltpêtrière Hospital and primarily a business zone; Massena, a mixed-use quarter which includes a number of historic industrial buildings scheduled for retention and rehabilitation, and a new *pole* (satellite campus) of the University of Paris with 20,000 students, west of the Perrault library; and Tolbiac, around the Bibliothèque Nationale and the first quarter to be developed (from 1992–2000). By 1999, 700 apartments in Tolbiac were occupied and nearly 3000 people were working in offices there. Eight more office buildings were also under construction.

The Seine Rive-Gauche project has involved the use of competitions, as is usual in France, for all major components. Amongst the practices responsible for completed buildings or working on projects for the area are those of Francis Soler, Jean-Michel Wilmotte, Christian de Portzamparc, Paul Chemetov, Paul Andreu, Antoine Grumbach and Dominique Perrault – a representative list of the leaders of the French profession. Within the next few years, it should be apparent whether the masterplan has produced not just an orderly and convenient urban environment but also one which draws on the genius of historic Paris and will become as much a part of the capital as the boulevards of Haussmann.

GRONINGEN
Groninger Museum

(1988-94)

Museums – and particularly art museums – have become key icons of the new urbanism, resources and points of reference in the competitive world of urban renewal and renaissance at the beginning of the new millennium. Most famously, Frank Gehry's Bilbao Guggenheim has demonstrated the power of a single 'object' building to transform the fortunes of a city (and even a region).

The Groninger Museum, close to the central railway station in this innovative and ambitious Dutch city, is, however, not so much an object as a complex of buildings, a city in miniature in its own right. The project, conceived by museum director Frans Haks, was made possible only through the financial support of Nederlandse Gasunie (Dutch Gas), whose vast headquarters is located in Groningen. It certainly represented an attempt to redefine the museum and, in the process, to redefine the place of culture in the modern city.

The museum was to be relocated from its old premises on the Praediniussingel to a new site by the canal on the Zwaaikom, on an artificial island/bridge, seen as a gateway between the historic core of the city and the 19th- and 20th-century quarters beyond. The scenario for the new building was established by Alessandro Mendini of Atelier Mendini (and late of Memphis), who had to address the issue of housing the very diverse collections of the museum (ranging from ancient Eastern artefacts to late 20th-century painting) – as well as galleries, the usual lecture hall, café, shop, library and administrative offices had to be provided.

Alessandro Mendini has explained that the project 'treats the Groningen museum as a possible urban utopia, as an ideal place abounding in surprises, an organic mental labyrinth that only indirectly demonstrates its didactic purposes'. The building, says Mendini, reflects 'the problematical junction between academy and avant-garde'. Such an approach had been specifically sought by Frans Haks, who (impressed by Disneyland and opposed to the elitism of traditional museums) wanted to

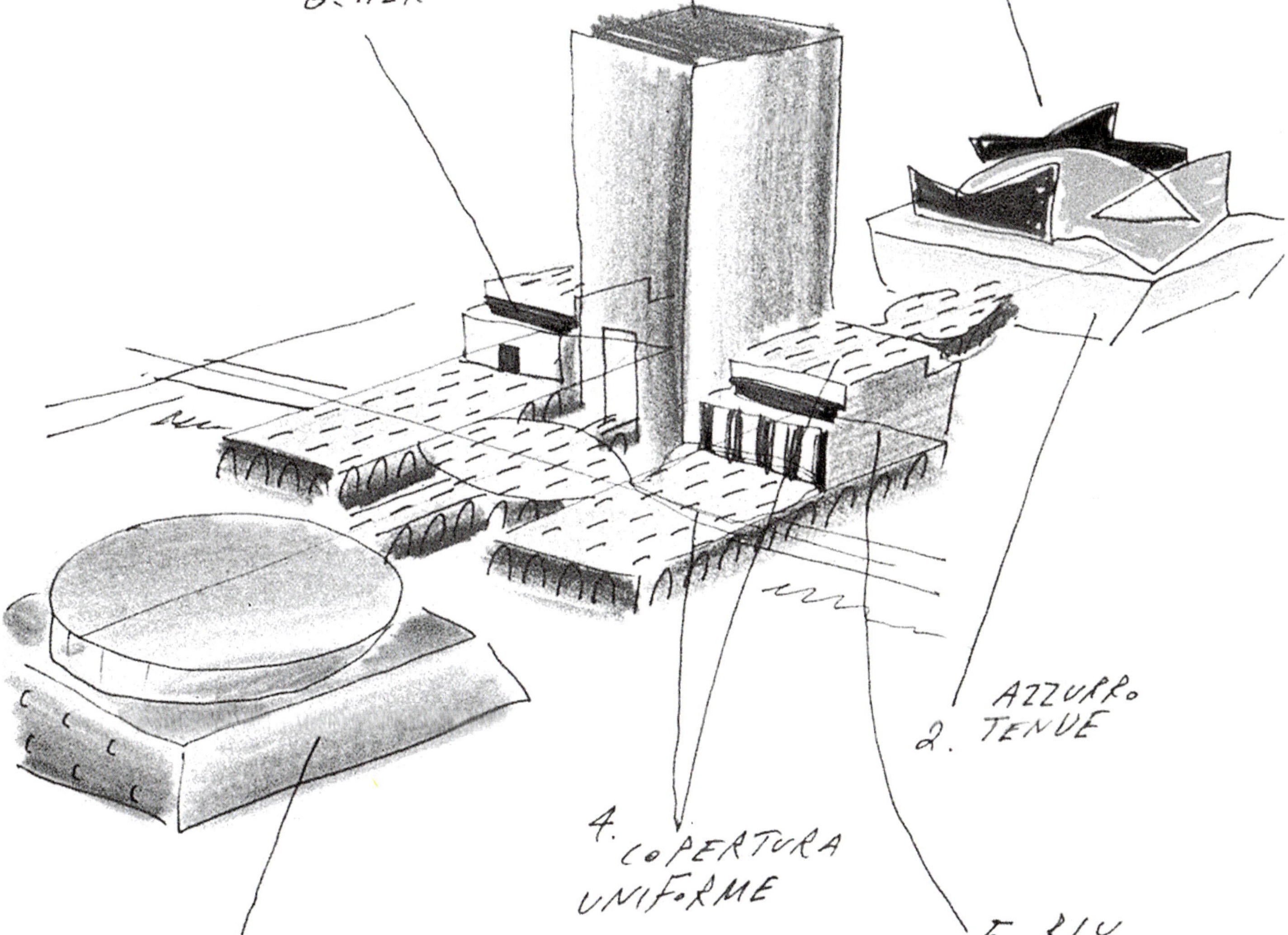

1. COLORI <OLLO>
   STELLA

3. ORO

VETRO
6. NERO

AZZURRO
2. TENUE

4. COPERTURA
   UNIFORME

5. BLU
   KLEIN

7. ROSA
   TENUE

attract new audiences, but it posed the problem of finding an alternative to the conventional *enfilade* of galleries, each devoted to a different period or medium. Instead, Mendini offered visitors, who might simply be *en route* from the station to the old town, the chance to dip into the collections, see only what they wanted, not be routemarched through room after room of artefacts. The museum is actually spread across three islands, linked by bridges. Mendini's 60-metre (200-foot) tower fills the central island and contains most of the museum's ancillary facilities, plus its store – the gold cladding symbolizes its role as a treasury. The west pavilion is in two parts, a brick-clad base by

Coop Himmelblau's rooftop pavilion (covered in rusting steel plates) is perhaps the most remarkable component in the complex.

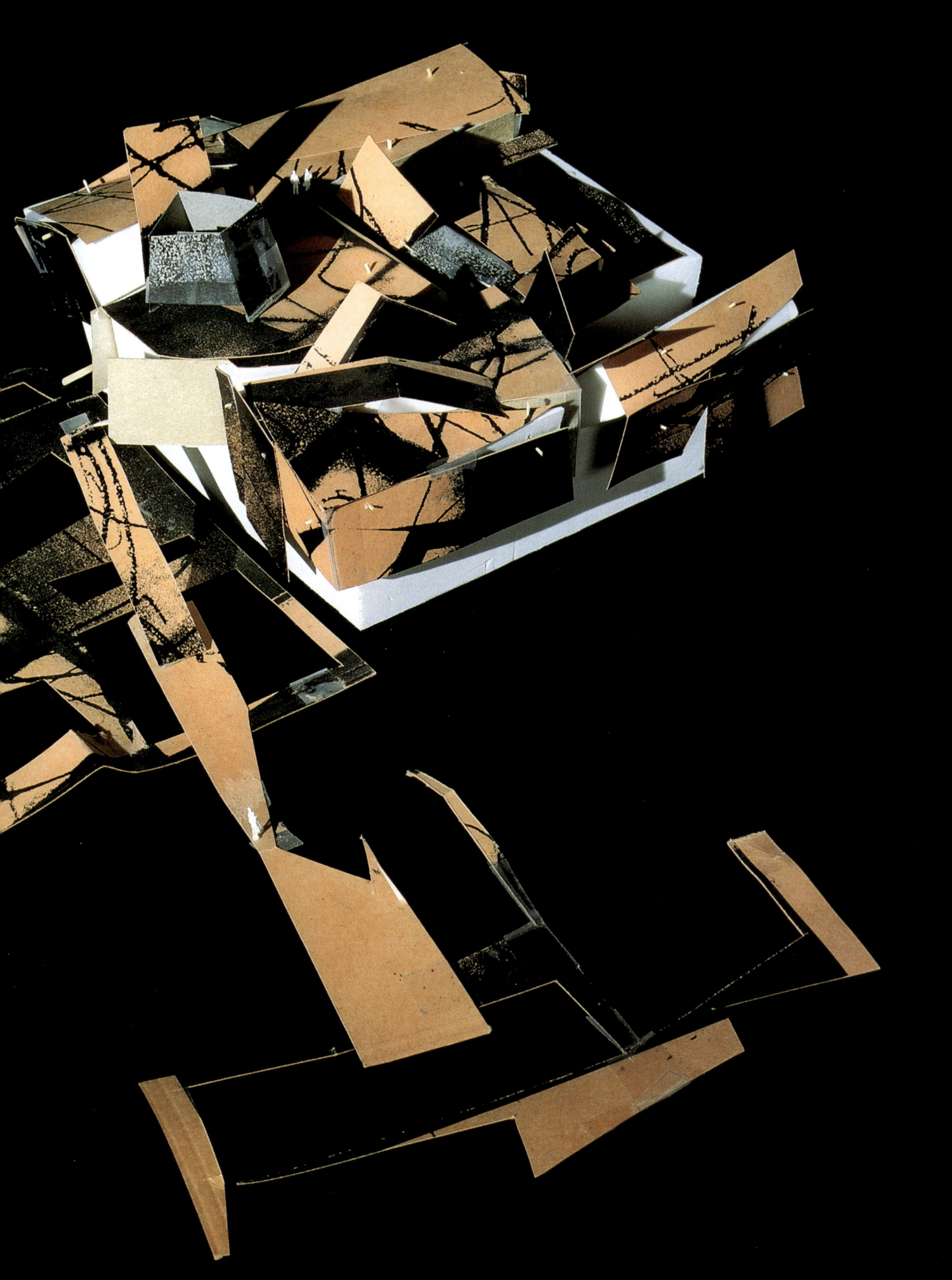

left
Coop Himmelblau's contribution to the museum complex is undoubtedly the most forceful element of the composition, externally and internally.

below
Scope is found in the masterplan for this striking aluminium-clad drum design by Philippe Starck, housing the museum's ceramics collection.

left and right
The warm and
colourful entrance
hall and stairwell of
Mendini's central
tower provide a
marked contrast to
the stark
utilitarianism of
Himmelblau's rooftop
eastern pavilion.

below
Mendini's initial
sketches for the
museum address themes
ranging from thought
to melancholy and
madness.

Michele De Lucchi, housing archaeology and local history, with Philippe Starck's circular Asian decorative arts gallery squatting on top. The eastern pavilion (contemporary art), designed by Mendini and covered in coloured laminate, in turn supports the most remarkable element of the complex, the rooftop pavilion (containing, oddly, historic pictures) by Coop Himmelblau. Clad in (rusting) steel plates and largely prefabricated in a Dutch shipyard, the pavilion is a looming and dynamic – perhaps even threatening – presence. It is this element in the scheme that gives the museum its ship-like quality and signals its serious challenge to conventional ideas of permanence and monumentality, not only as applied to the world of museums but to urban architecture more generally.

...THOUGHT...

...MADNESS...

...MELANCOLY...

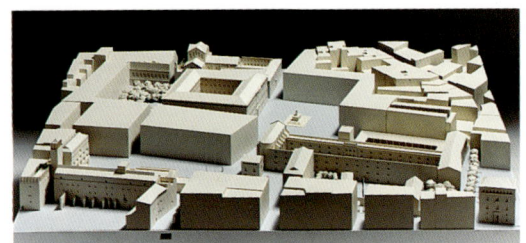

BARCELONA
Raval district and
Contemporary Art
Museum

(1985-99)

Barcelona's rise from regional capital to world city took place within the space of two decades, with the 1992 Olympic Games as a landmark event in the process of regeneration and renaissance. The reassertion of the public domain has been fundamental throughout – as the Barcelona architect Oriol Bohigas insists, 'the public space is the city'. At the end of the 19th century, Barcelona underwent a massive expansion in line with the urban masterplan of Ildefons Cerda – the Cerda grid provided a disciplined framework for rapid growth. Today, all-embracing plans of this kind are discredited and, in any case, massive extensions of Barcelona's built-up area are not envisaged. Instead, the city has concentrated on developing a series of masterplans for distinct quarters, with architecture leading the way rather than taking a subsidiary role.

A further ingredient in the Barcelona approach has been a strong emphasis on the cultural dimension of the city, so that the commission (in 1980) of Lluis Clotet's practice to examine the potential for renewal of the Raval district was linked from the start to the arts and education. The Raval lies west of the Ramblas at the heart of the historic city – the famous Liceu opera house (recently reconstructed after a devastating fire) and the much-loved Boqueria market are nearby. The Raval was an area of convents, established there between the 14th and 18th centuries. When the religious orders were expropriated in 1837, their buildings found new uses as schools and charitable institutions, but by the second half of the 20th century the general picture in the Raval was one of steady decline and under-occupation. Its narrow alleys were avoided by the crowds streaming along the Ramblas and the area was seen as unsavoury and dangerous.

Clotet was asked to look at potential uses for a number of historic buildings there, with the Casa de la Caritat and Casa de la Misericordia already identified as the possible home of a new cultural centre. The resulting masterplan, approved in 1985, has formed the basis for the ongoing renewal of the area. A

The way in which new architecture and rehabilitation can work in harmony to regenerate rundown city areas is demonstrated in the Raval quarter of Barcelona (masterplan shown right) - the restored Casa de la Caritat (top right) forms a group with Richard Meier's new Museum of Contemporary Art.

Meier's museum is
contextually
responsive in scale
and orientation, and
plays an important
role in giving this
area of the city
centre a new role.
Its cool white
appearance, typical
of Meier's work,
looks surprisingly at
home in this medieval
quarter.

basic requirement was a strategy for access and for public space, since the narrow streets of the quarter were unsuitable for modern traffic. The emphasis has been on pedestrian circulation, with a series of new squares and parks created, though some new parking has been provided, underground and at street level. Some demolition has been necessary to improve access and open up new public spaces. Clotet's proposals included the conversion of the Casa de la Caritat to gallery and theatre use, and of the Misericordia to use by the university.

The decision to construct a new Museum of Contemporary Art in this area has transformed a forgotten quarter into a much-frequented visitor attraction. Completed in 1995, Richard Meier's Museum is international both in the quality of the environment and facilities which it offers and, superficially at least, in its aesthetic. The building is, however, subtly contextual in terms of its response to the surrounding area and to the refurbished historic buildings. Its ground floor is part of a pedestrian pattern which extends across the whole quarter. Meier works with the city, in the spirit of the new Barcelona – part of the formula which has made his office so prominent a contributor to the European, as much as the American, urban scene.

Modern rooftop additions to the Convent dels Angels (adjacent to the Contemporary Art Museum) by Clotet, Paricio and Associates provide both a shady retreat (left) and a stunning view of the city (above and right).

ROTTERDAM
Schouwburgplein

(1992-7)

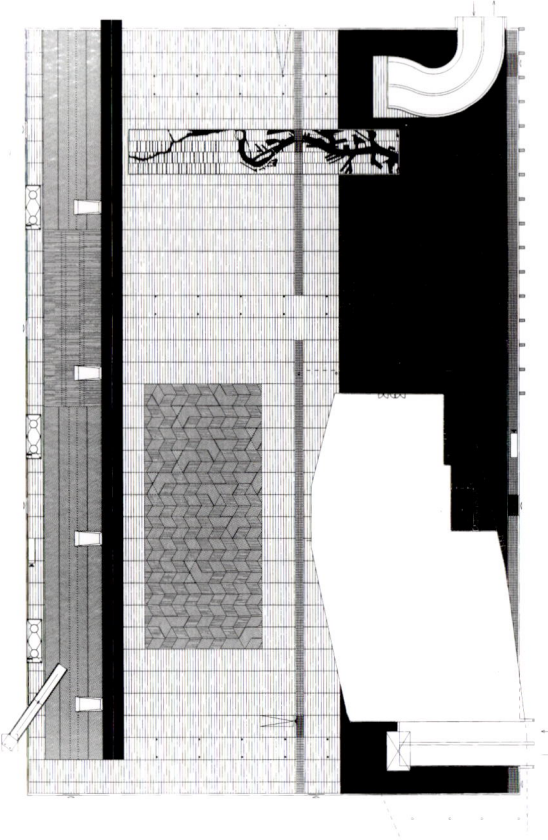

The Schouwburgplein is a prominent public space in Rotterdam, a city heroically, but facelessly, reconstructed after devastation in the Second World War and with a rather depressing run of 1980s commercial blocks. The square's central position, close to the main shopping and office areas of the city and the Central Station, focussed attention on its poor condition – it was actually laid out on top of a 1960s underground carpark – and led to the 1990 project by West 8 architects (with Adriaan Geuze) to radically reconfigure it.

Significantly, Rotterdam's City Theatre (Schouwburg – hence the name of the square), temporarily rehoused after the war, had finally been rebuilt in 1982–8 on the south side of the Schouwburgplein, facing a Sixties concert hall on the north side. The depressing state of the space in front of the theatre was seen as increasingly incongruous in a prestigious cultural quarter.

The existence of the subterranean parking posed problems for the architects, since the roof of the garage was insufficiently strong to carry heavy paving. In response, West 8 proposed an ultra-light new surface in the form of a raised (350 millimetres/13 ¾ inches) deck constructed out of a mix of materials – epoxy, metal, timber and rubber – designed to reflect the mix of activities in the space. Equally, the ventilation towers of the carpark had to be retained – they have been reclad and used to display a digital clock and advertising. At night, they are dramatically lit.

West 8's scheme (radically re-designed after Koen van Nelsen's Pathé multiplex cinema was first proposed in 1992) makes an inert space into an open air stage, a place for performances and for people. The essence of the scheme is changeability – lighting and, in summer, water jets transform its identity. Highly sculptural lighting gantries, 35 metres (115 feet) high, are another ingredient – they change position hourly and the public can set them in motion by inserting a coin. In contrast to more traditional squares, this is a space where the user has an element of control.

top left
The Schouwburgplein's setting is central to Rotterdam, but its architectural context of 1980s commercial blocks is mundane.

left and right
The surfacing of the square is a lightweight, layered, raised deck, designed to be used for performances.

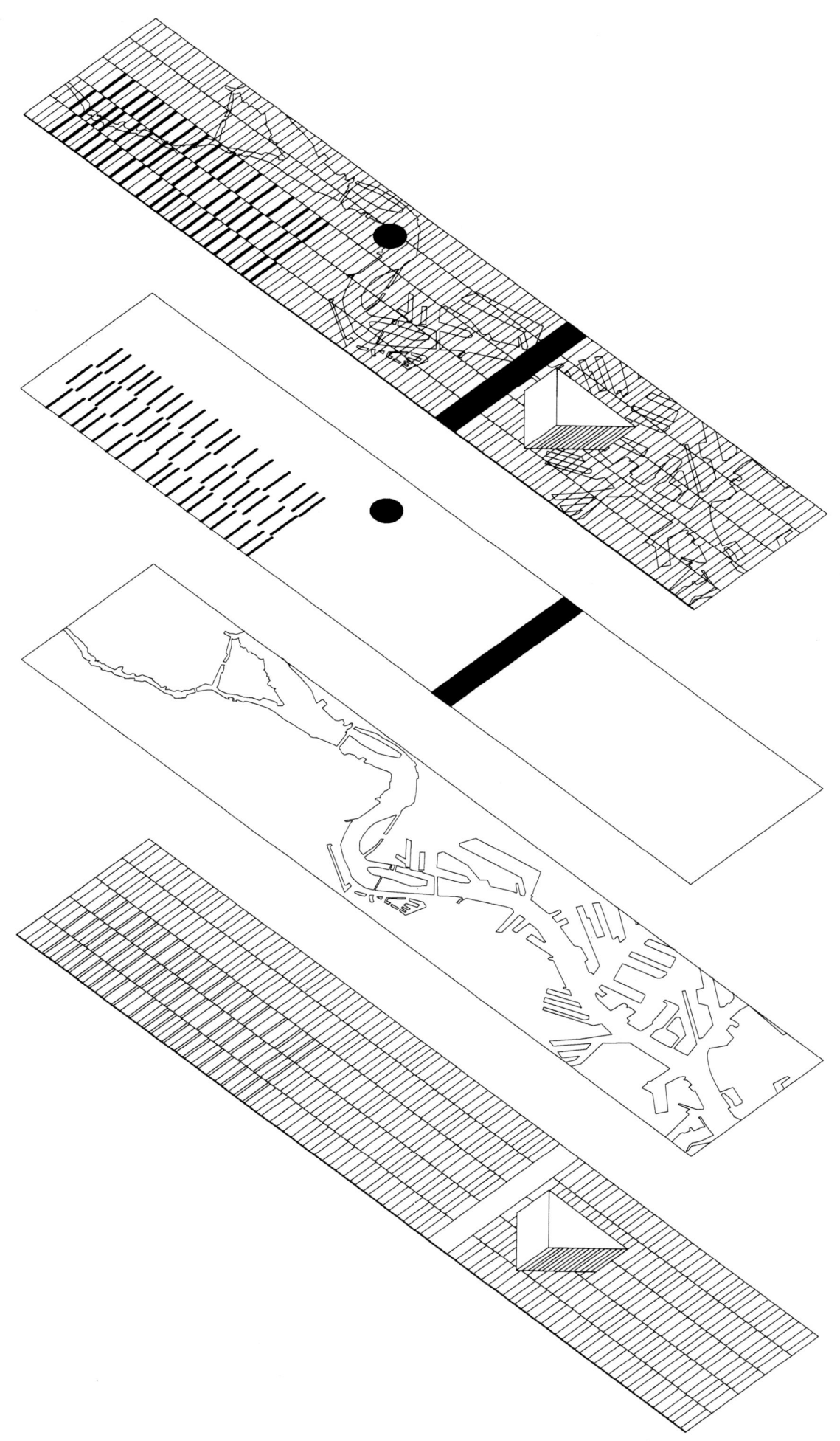

Rotterdam

The van Nelsen multiplex (with seven screens) also sits on top of the underground parking, so that the structure had to be extremely lightweight. The cinema invades the square, reducing its area, but its foyer is treated as an extension of the external space, essentially public in character. The cinema spaces are really no more than closed boxes, but van Nelsen has given the building a memorable form by enveloping them in a flowing container, formed out of polycarbonate sheeting, accommodating circulation areas and cafes. (When illuminated after dark, the building has been compared to a Japanese paper lamp.) The decision to approve the cinema project was widely criticized as a sell-out of public space to commerce, invalidating the landscaping scheme. Oddly, the net result of this 'compromise' has been to create a more intense space in which landscape and architecture work in harmony. The project accepts the nature of the post-war city – you can hardly ignore the high-rise blocks that press in on every side. It is essentially pragmatic and notable for its (structural and fiscal) economy, but its frank appeal to a more youthful and mobile vision of urban culture than that embodied in the concert hall and theatre have ensured its instant success.

The space is animated with moveable lighting gantries and the dramatically reclad ventilation towers which service the existing subterranean carpark. The foyer of van Nelsen's Pathé cinema (below) provides an extension of the public space.

At night, movement, light and sound activate what was once an inert space (right). The position of the lighting can be controlled by the public at the drop of a coin (left).

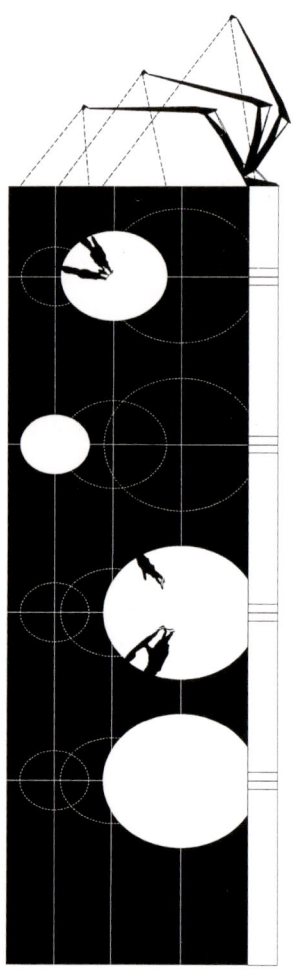

Project credits

Client
The City of Almere, MAB, Blauwhoed
Eurowoningen

Masterplan
OMA – Office for Metropolitan Architecture

**Car Park, Architect 'blok 6' (Multiplex
Cinema, Foodcourt, Stores)**
OMA – Office for Metropolitan Architecture

Client
City of Arnhem

**Masterplan, Transfer Hall, Bus Terminal,
Train Stations, Tunnel Parking, offices
and shops**
Un Studio Ben Van Berkel & Bos BV in
collaboration with Ove Arup & Partners

Client
Battery Park City Authority

Masterplan
Battery Park City Authority

Battery Pointe Residential Unit
Bond Ryder James Architect

The Belvedere
Child Associates

Brookdale Senior Living Units
Schuman Lichtenstein Clamen & Efron;
Lucien La Grange & Associates

Cove Club
James Stewart Polshek & Partners Architects.

Embassy Suites Hotel and Movie Theatre
Perkins Eastman Architects

Hudson Tower Residential Unit
Davis Brody & Associates

Hudson View East Residential Unit
James Rossant Architects;
Mitchell/Giurgola Architects

**Liberty Court, House and Terrace
Residential Units**
Ulrich Franzen, The Vilkas Group;
James Stewart Polshek

Liberty View Residential Unit
Ehren Krantz, Eckstut & Khun

Museum of Jewish Heritage
Kevin Roche, John Dinkerloo and Associates

New York Mercantile Exchange
Skidmore, Owings & Merrill

Parc Place Residential Unit
Gruzen Samton

The Regatta
Gruzen Samton; James Stewart Polshek
& Partners Architects

Residential Units
Hardy Holzmann Pfeiffer Associates; Davis
Brody Bond

River Rose Block – Rector Place
Neighborhood: Rothzeid, Kaiserman, Thomson
& Bee Architects

Soundings Residential Unit
Bond Ryder James

Stuyvestant School
Gruzen Samton

Tribeca Bridge
Skidmore, Owings & Merrill with Signe Nielsen
(landscape architect)

Tribeca Parc
Robert Stern Architects; Costas Kondylis
and Associates

Tribeca Pointe
Gruzen Samton

Tribeca Tower and Tribeca Bridge Tower
Pasenella & Klein, Stoltzman & Berg; Costas
Kondylis and Associates; Richard Cook &
Associates

World Financial Centre
Cesar Pelli & Associates

Robert F. Wagnar, Jr. Park
Olin Partnership (Landscape Architect);
Machado & Silvetti (Architects and Urban
Designers); Lynden Miller (Garden Designer)

BILBAO METRO AND ABANDO INTERCHANGE, SPAIN

Client
Bilbao Ria 2000 Consortium

Masterplan of the Abandoibarra
Cesar Pelli & Associates; Balmori Associates,
Eugenio Aguinaga

Abando Passenger Interchange
Michael Wilford & Partners

Campo Volantin Footbridge
Calatrava Valls

Congress and Concert Hall
Federico Soriano, Colores Palacios with Carlos
Arroyo, Alberto Nicolau, Anoel Verdasco

Guggenheim Museum
Frank O. Gehry & Associates

Metro
Foster & Partners

Sondika Airport
Calatrava Valls

CANARY WHARF DEVELOPMENT, LONDON, UK

Client
Canary Wharf Limited

Housing Units
Ralph Erskine

**Canary Wharf Tower, Retail and Assembly
Building; Docklands Light Railway Station;
Citibank Tower**
Cesar Pelli & Associates Inc.; **Associate
Architect:** Adamson Associates

**Citibank Headquarters; Hong Kong and
Shanghai Banking Corporation London
Headquarters; Canary Wharf Station**
Foster & Partners

CHIADO DISTRICT DEVELOPMENT, LISBON, PORTUGAL

Client
Department of Municipal Works, Lisbon

Masterplan
Alvaro Siza - Arquitecto

Engineer
Structure STA - Segadaes Tavares

Associados Lda

Landscape Architects
Joao Gomes da Silva

General Contractor
Several Contractors

Construction Manager
Cabinete de Recuperaçao do Chiado

COLUMBUS INTERNATIONAL EXPOSITION, GENOA, ITALY

Client
Commune of Genoa

**Masterplan (Congress Hall, Cinema,
Aquarium, Exhibition Area, Offices,
Commercial Centres, Ice Rink (winter);
Open Theatre (summer), Restaurants, Gym,
Swimming Pool)**
Renzo Piano Building Workshop

Collaborators
R. Melai; E. Miola

Planning
Tekne Planning

Consultant
F. Pagnano

Contractor and Management
Italimpianti

FRANKFURT 21 AND STATION QUARTER, FRANKFURT, GERMANY

Client
Deutsche Bahn AG

Masterplan
gmp – von Gerkan Marg und Partner architekten

Consultant Urban Planner
AS & P, Prof. A. Speer

Landscape Architect
Wehberg, Eppinger, Schmidtke

GRONINGER CITY MUSEUM, GRONINGEN, THE NETHERLANDS

Client
Foundation for the Construction of the New Groningen Museum

Architectural Project
Alessandro Mendini, Francesco Mendini, Alchimia

Guest Architects
Philippe Starck, Coop Himmelblau, Michele De Lucchi

Executive Development and Works Management
Team 4

Economy and Construction Management
Twijnstra

Structural Project
Ingenieursbureau Wassenaar BV

Technical Systems
Van Heugten BV

INNER HARBOUR, DUISBURG, GERMANY

Steiger Schwanentour, Harbour Promenade, Hafenforum and canals

Client
Innenhafen Duisburg Entwicklungsgesellschaft mbH

Developer and Project Manager
LEG Landesentwicklungsgesellschaft Nordrhein-Westfalen GmbH

Design
Foster & Partners

Civil Engineer
Hans Kolbeck

Pontoon Engineer
Ingenieursbüro Klement

M&E Pavilion
ITG

Dam

Design
Foster & Partners

Engineer
Spiekermann GmbH & Co.

Canals

Design
Foster & Partners

Water Engineering & Project Management
Abdou GmbH

Structural Engineer
Ingenieursbüro R. Knoke

Civil Engineer
Bplan Ingenieursgesellschaft

KOP VAN ZUID HARBOUR REDEVELOPMENT, ROTTERDAM, THE NETHERLANDS

Client
Rotterdam City Municipalities

Masterplan
OMA – Office for Metropolitan Architecture;
City Planners (Kop Van Zuid); Foster & Partners
(Whilhemina Pier); Bolles-Wilson with DS+U
(Landing Square and Surrounds)

Bridge
Un Studio Ben Van Berkel & Bos BV

Hotel New York
Dorine de Vos, Hans Loos, Daan van der Have

Mixed-use Building
OMA – Office for Metropolitan Architecture

**Quay Landscaping and Bridgewatcher's
House; New Luxor Theatre, N.Y. Field**
Architekturburo Bolles-Wilson

Tower
Renzo Piano

HYOGO PREFECTURAL MUSEUM AND ROKKO HOUSING, KOBE, JAPAN

Client
Hyogo Prefecture

Hyogo Prefectural Museum of Modern Art;
Kobe Waterfront Plaza; Rokko Housing
Tadao Ando Architect & Associates

KUALA LUMPUR DEVELOPMENT, MALAYSIA

Phase I

Client
KLCC (Holdings) Berhad

KLCC Masterplan
Klages, Carter, Vail & Partners

Petronas Towers
Cesar Pelli & Associates Inc.; KLCC Architects

Suria KLCC
Cesar Pelli & Associates Inc; Walker Group

Menara Maxis
Kevin Roche, John Dinkeloo and Associates

Menara ESSO
Kumpulas Senireka Sdn. Bhd.

Mandarin Oriental Kuala Lumpur Hotel
Wimberly, Allison, Tong & Goo; Group
Design Parternship

KLCC Park
Burle Marx & CIA. Ltda; KLCC Architects

The District Cooling Centre
KLCC Architects

The Asy-Syakirin Mosque
KLCC Architects

PUTRAJAYA NEW CAPITAL CONCEPT

Malaysian Government Project Concept
consortium of architectural consultancies

Cyber Jaya Intelligent City
Malaysian Government proposal

**Multimedia Super Corridor (MSC);
Eco-Media City**
Kisho Kurokawa; BEP Akitek

INDEPENDENT DEVELOPMENTS
IN KUALA LUMPUR

Kuala Lumpur International Airport

Kisho Kurokawa with Akitek Jururancang
(Malysia Sdn Bhd); BDG McColl (detailed
interior design); Arklandskap (landscape
design)

Central Plaza

T. R. Hamzah & Yeang Sdn Bhd

HONG KONG CHEK LAP KOK AIRPORT
AND KOWLOON STATION, CHINA

Chek Lap Kok Airport

Client

Hong Kong Airport Authority

Architects

Foster & Partners; Mott Consortium (Architects
and Designers); Mott Connell Ltd. (Engineering
and Project Management); BAA plc (Airport
Planning, Operational Systems and Group
Technical Services)

**Mass Transit Railway Station; Kowloon
Ventilation Building; Landmark Tower**

Client

Mass Transit Railway Corporation

Architect

Terry Farrell & Partners

**Authorized Person and Collaborating
Architects**

station: Ho & Partners; property: Kwan &
Associates; Leigh and Orange; Dennis Lau & Ng
Chun Man

LINK QUAY DEVELOPMENT,
SANTA CRUZ, TENERIFE,
CANARY ISLANDS

Client

Port Authority of Santa Cruz

Masterplan

Herzog and De Meuron

POTSDAMER PLATZ; THE REICHSTAG
AND GOVERNMENT BUILDINGS,
BERLIN, GERMANY

Client

Daimler Benz AG

POTSDAMER PLATZ

Masterplan

Renzo Piano Building Workshop; C. Kohlbecker

**Debis Tower; Imax-Theatre; Residential;
Units; Spielbank; Musical Theatre**

Renzo Piano Building Workshop/C. Kohlbecker

**Daimler Benz; Headquarters of the
Berliner Volksbank**

Arata Isozaki & Associates; Steffen Lehmann
Architekten BDA

Sony Centre

Murphy/Jahn

Daimler Chrysler

Richard Rogers Partnership

Residential Units

Richard Rogers Partnership; Lauber & Wohr

Offices

Richard Rogers Partnership; Jose Rafael Moneo;
Hans Kollhoff

Hyatt Hotel

Jose Rafael Moneo

Multiplex Cinema, CinemaxX

Lauber & Wohr

NEW PARLIAMENT
AND GOVERNMENT DISTRICT

Client
The Federal Republic of Germany represented by Bundesbaugesellschaft Berlin mbH.

Masterplan
Charlotte Frank

Federal Chancellery
Axel Schultes

THE REICHSTAG

Client
The Federal Republic of Germany represented by Bundesbaugesellschaft Berlin mbH

Architect
Foster & Partners

RAVAL DISTRICT REHABILITATION,
BARCELONA, SPAIN

Client
Architecture and Housing Department of the Ministry for Public Works and Urban Development

Masterplan
The Lluís Clotet Group (Alfons Guiu, Pepe Zazurca, Angel Orbananos, Lluís Clotet, Pepita Teixidor, Oscar Tusquets)

CCCB
Viaplana/Pinon

Convent dels Angels
Clotet, Paricio I Assoc.

Museum of Contemporary Art
Richard Meier

ROYAL OPERA HOUSE, LONDON, UK

Client
Royal Opera House

Architects
Dixon Jones BDP (Limited Company formed from Jeremy Dixon, Edward Jones and BDP Partnership)

Interior Design Adviser (Auditorium)
Mlinaric Henry & Zervudachi

Historic Buildings Adviser (Auditorium)
Margaret & Richard Davies and Associates

Construction Manager
Schal Construction Management

External Envelope Consultant
Arup Façade Engineering

Theatre Design Consultant
Anne Minors

Technical Consultant
Haddon Few Montuschi; Duncan Few

Structural and Services Engineering
Ove Arup and Partners

Acoustic Engineer
Arup Acoustics

Theatre Consultant
ROH Theatre Consultants

Construction Adviser
Stanhope Properties

SAIGON SOUTH MASTERPLAN, HO CHI MINH CITY, VIETNAM

Client
Phu My Hung Corporation, Ho Chi Minh City

Developers
Phu My Hung Development Corporation (PMH); Tan Thuan Industrial Promotion Company; CT&D Group

Masterplan/Urban Designers
Skidmore, Owings & Merrill, International Ltd.

Architects
Koetter Kim & Associates (urban design);
Kenzo Tange Associates (urban design);
Yu Wang Design C. Ltd. (urban design);
Barton-Aschman Associates (traffic);
Moh and Associates International, Ltd. (civil);
EBASCO-CTCI (electrical)

SCHOUWBURGPLEIN, ROTTERDAM, THE NETHERLANDS

Client
City Council of Rotterdam

Masterplan
West 8 Landscape Architects, Adriaan Geuze

Multiplex Cinema Complex
Koen van Nelsen

SEATTLE DOWNTOWN DEVELOPMENT AND WATERFRONT REGENERATION, USA

Client
City of Seattle, Washington, under the auspices of Mayor Paul Schell

Music Experience
Frank O. Gehry Architects

Civic Centre
Hewitt Architects; Weinstein Copeland Architects

Football/Soccer Stadium and Exhibition Centre
Ellerbee Becket in association with Loschky Marquardt Nesholm; Developer
First & Goal Inc.

Safeco Field Baseball Stadium; Headquarters of Vulcan Northwest; Pacific Place Mall; Swedish Medical Centre Southeast Wing Addition; Seattle-Tacoma International Airport (2002); The Federal Courthouse (2004)
NBBJ

Renovation of Union Station
NBBJ; Landscape Architects: Murase Associates

King Street Station
Otak Inc. Associate Architect
Hardy Holzman Pfeiffer

Nordstrom Flagship Store; Convention Place (offices); W Hotel; Westlake Towers high rise blocks; Space Needle Renovation
Callison Architecture

Millennium Tower; Madison Financial Tower
Zimmer Gunsul Frasca

'Harbor Steps' Residential Units; Central Waterfront Project/Bell Street Pier
Hewitt Architects

SEINE RIVE-GAUCHE DEVELOPMENT, PARIS, FRANCE

Clients
Various, including public housing firms, private developers, public administrations, state institutions

Project control
Société d'Economie Mixte d'Aménagement de Paris – SEMAPA

Masterplan – Austerlitz Area
Christian Devillers; Jacques Lucan

Offices
Christian Hauvette

Masterplan – Tolbiac Area
Roland Schweitzer

Housing
Philippe Gazeau; Jérome Brunet and Eric Saunier; Francis Soler; Jean-Pierre Buffi; Pierre Gagnet; Georges Maurios; Jacques Ripault and Denise Duhart; Acaur – René Verlha

School and Housing
Philippe Barthélémy and Sylvia Grino

Offices: SANOFI
Gilles Thin, Franco Cianfaglione and Benoît Graveraux

Gardens
Cabinet Arpage, Paul Brichet; Michel Desvigne and Christine Dalnoky

Film Theatre Complex MK2
Jean-Michel Wilmotte; Frédéric Namur

Masterplan – Massena Area
Christian de Portzamparc

High School
Paul Chemetov and Borja Huidobro

Capital and Continental Offices
Robert Turner – ARTE, Jean-Marie Charpentier

Masterplan – Rue de Chevaleret Area
Bruno Fortier

Avenue de France
Paul Andreu; Jean-Michel Wilmotte

SNCF Works
Jean-Marie Duthilleul; Etienne Tricaud, François
Pradillon

RATP Works (Météor)
Antoine Grumbach; Pierre Schall

New French National Library
Dominique Perrault

Charles de Gaulle Bridge
Louise Arretche; Roman Karasinski

Planted Walk
François Grether; Jacqueline Osty

STUTTGART STATION QUARTER AND AVENUE 21, GERMANY

Client:
Deutsche Bahn AG

Masterplan
gmp – von Gerkan Marg und Partner
Architekten

Freiraumplaner
Wehberg.Eppinger.Schmidtke

Statik Bahnhof
Schlaich, Bergermann & Partner

TEMPLE BAR, DUBLIN, IRELAND

Client
Temple Bar Properties Ltd.

Framework Plan
Group 91 Architects (Shay Cleary Architects;
Grafton Architects; Paul Keogh Architects;
McCullough Mulvin Architects; McGarry
NiEanaigh Architects; O'Donnell & Tuomey
Architects; Shane O'Toole Architect; Derek
Tynan Architects)

Arthouse (curved street)
Shay Cleary Architects

Temple Bar Square (including apartment/restaurant building onto square)
Grafton Architects

Gaity School of Acting and Meeting House Square
Paul Keogh Architects

The Music Centre; independent project carried out in the Temple Bar Area; Black Church Print Studios; Temple Bar Gallery and Studios
McCullough Mulvin Architects

Poddle Bridge
McGarry NiEanaigh Architects

Irish Film Centre; National Photographic Archive Gallery of Photography
O'Donnell & Tuomey Architects

The Ark (with Michael Kelly Architects)
Shane O'Toole

The Printworks
Derek Tynan Architects

VICTORY DISTRICT, DALLAS, USA

Client
Hillwood Development Company

Architecture Planning and Urban Design
Koetter, Kim and Associates

Consultant Architects
Charles F. McAfee; Good Fulton & Farrell
Architects

Site Planners and Landscape Architects
Rolland/Towers LLC

Landscape Architecture
MESA Design Group

Graphics and Signage
Gensler

Picture Credits

Courtesy Tadao Ando (74 top, 77)

Courtesy Battery Park Authority (134, 140 top –
Donald Penny)

Courtesy BDP (205)

Luc Boegly/Archipress (223 top, 227–229)

British Architectural Library – RIBA (9)

Richard Bryant/Arcaid (57, 101, 102, 144–145)

Courtesy Callison Architects (36 middle)

Courtesy Canary Wharf Ltd. (99 top, 100, 103,
104)

Lluís Casals (230–232, 233 bottom)

Peter Cook (60–65, 183)

Richard Davies (125, 159 bottom, 161)

Michel Denance (40)

Michel Denance/Archipress (45)

Franck Eustache/Archipress (19, 218–219, 221)

Courtesy Terry Farrell & Partners (180–181, 183
top, 186 top)

Courtesy Foster & Partners (105, 124–126 top,
128 top, 131 top, 158 bottom, 159 top)

Courtesy of Foreign Office Architects (16)

The Fotomas Index (7)

Scott Frances/ESTO (17, 233 top)

Chris Gascoigne (184–187)

Dennis Gilbert/VIEW (106–107, 174
bottom–178, 204–213)

Roland Halbe/Artur (42–43, 52 top)

Courtesy Herzog and de Meuron (150–153)

Courtesy Hewitt Architects (34–35)

Timothy Hursley (136)

Werner Huthmacher (46 bottom–49)

Kaori Ichikawa (74 top)

Martin Jones (80 bottom)

Katsuhisa Kida (50–51)

Index
of architects and projects

Published in the United States in 2000 by
te Neues Publishing Company
16 West 22nd Street
New York, NY 10010

Library of Congress Cataloging-in-Publication Data
is available.

ISBN 3-8238-5461-5

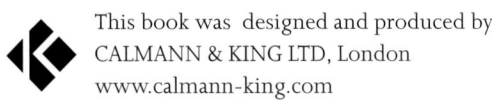 This book was designed and produced by
CALMANN & KING LTD, London
www.calmann-king.com

Designed by Isambard Thomas

Printed in China